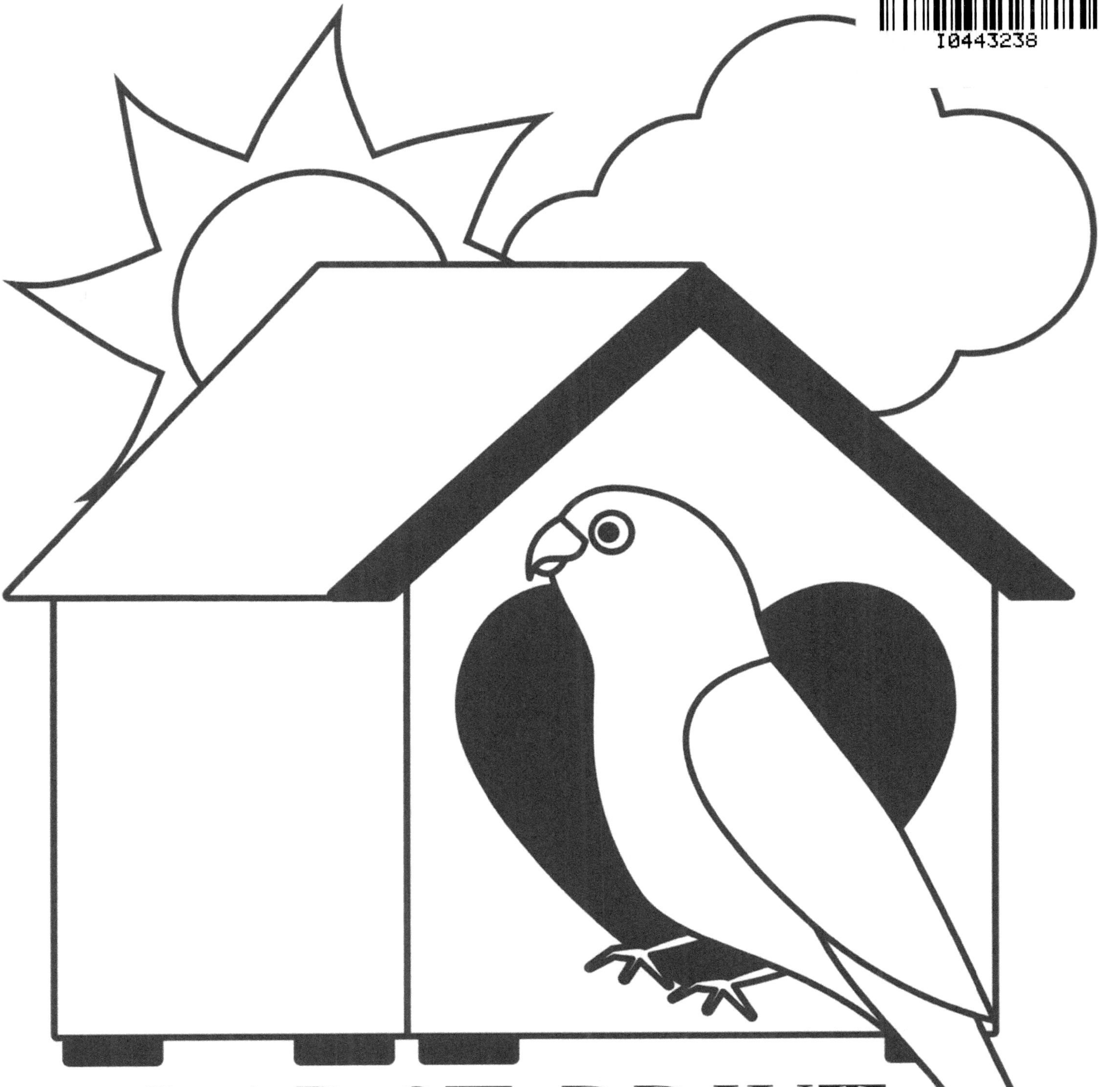

LARGE PRINT COLORING BOOK

ISBN: 9798585547928

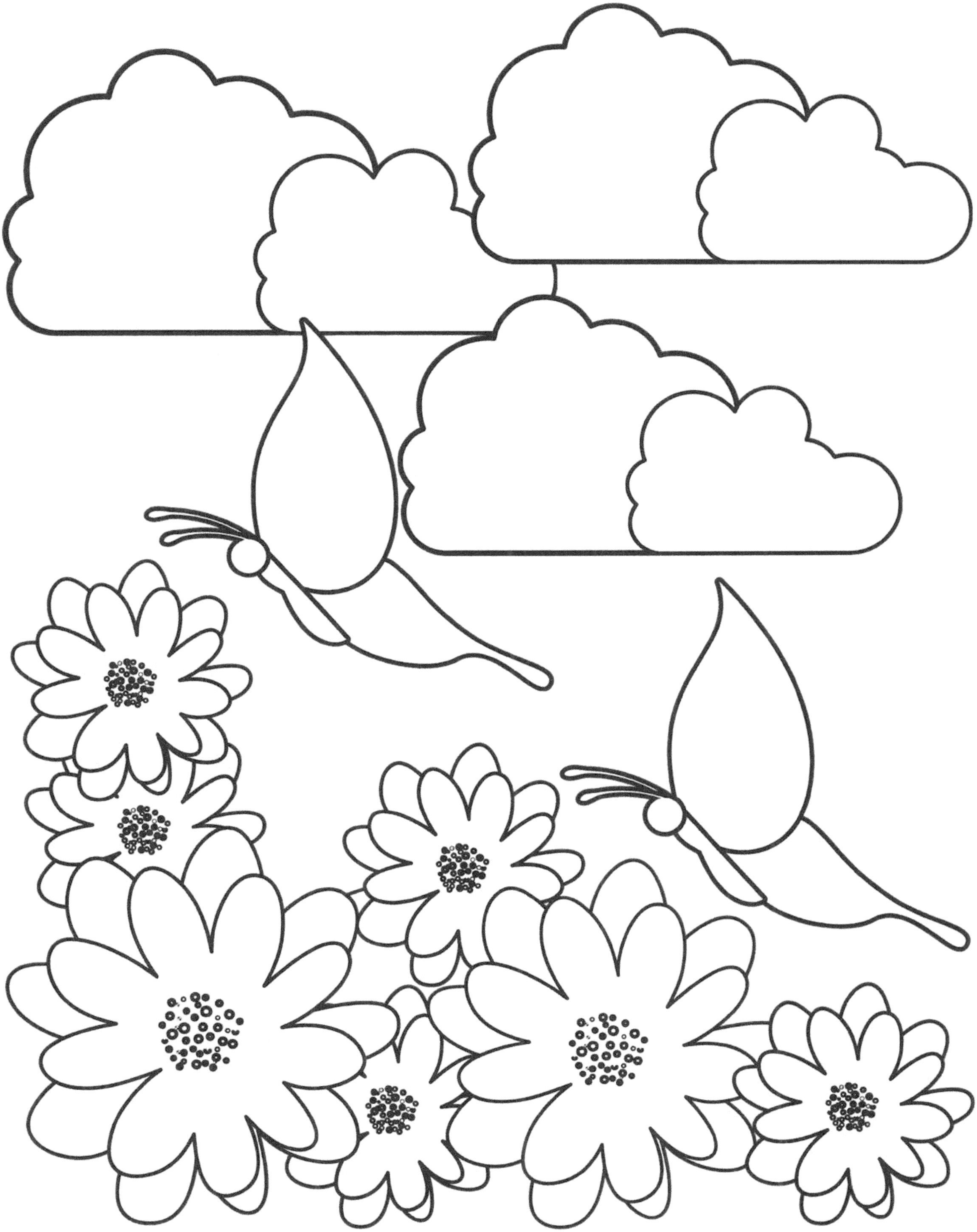

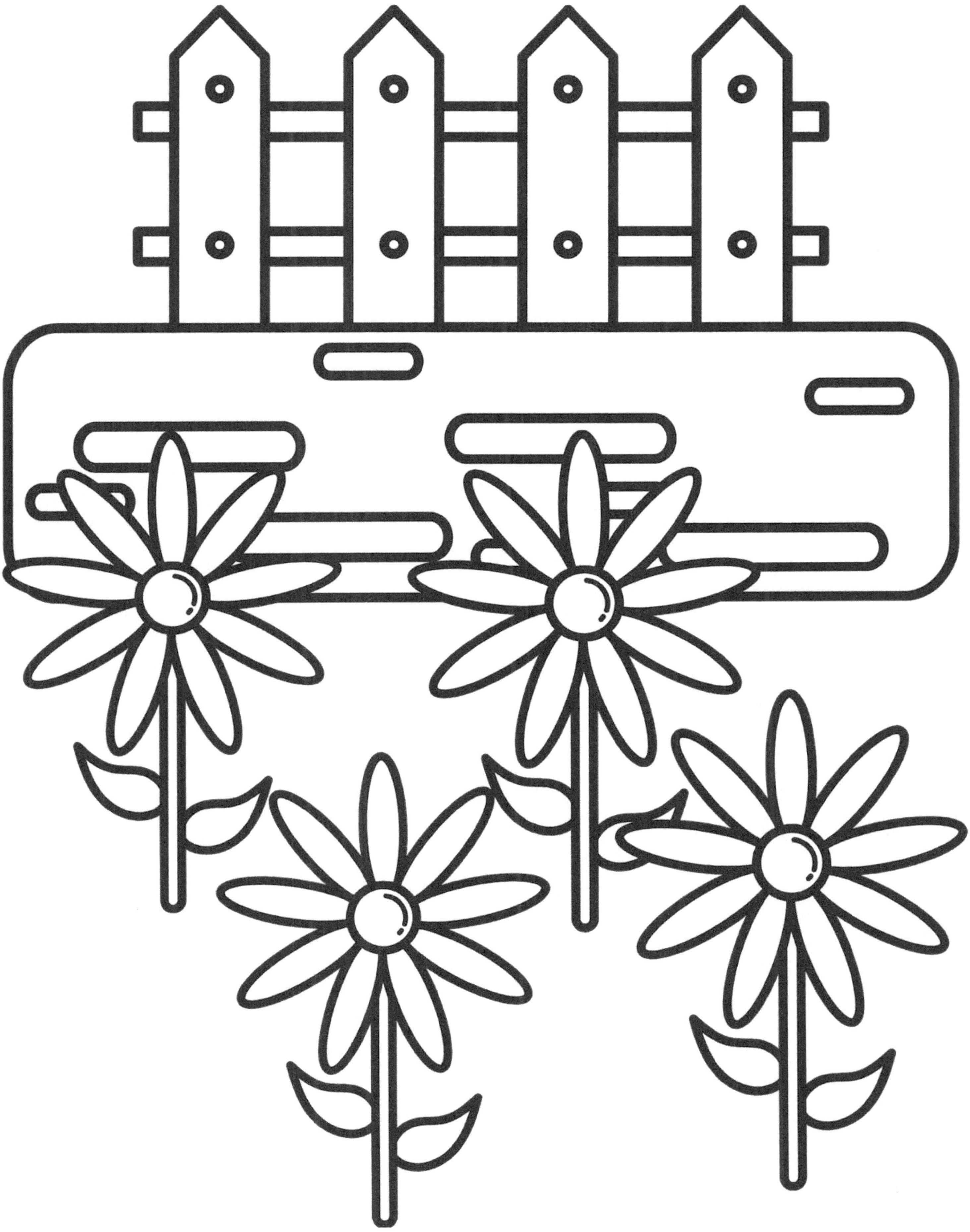

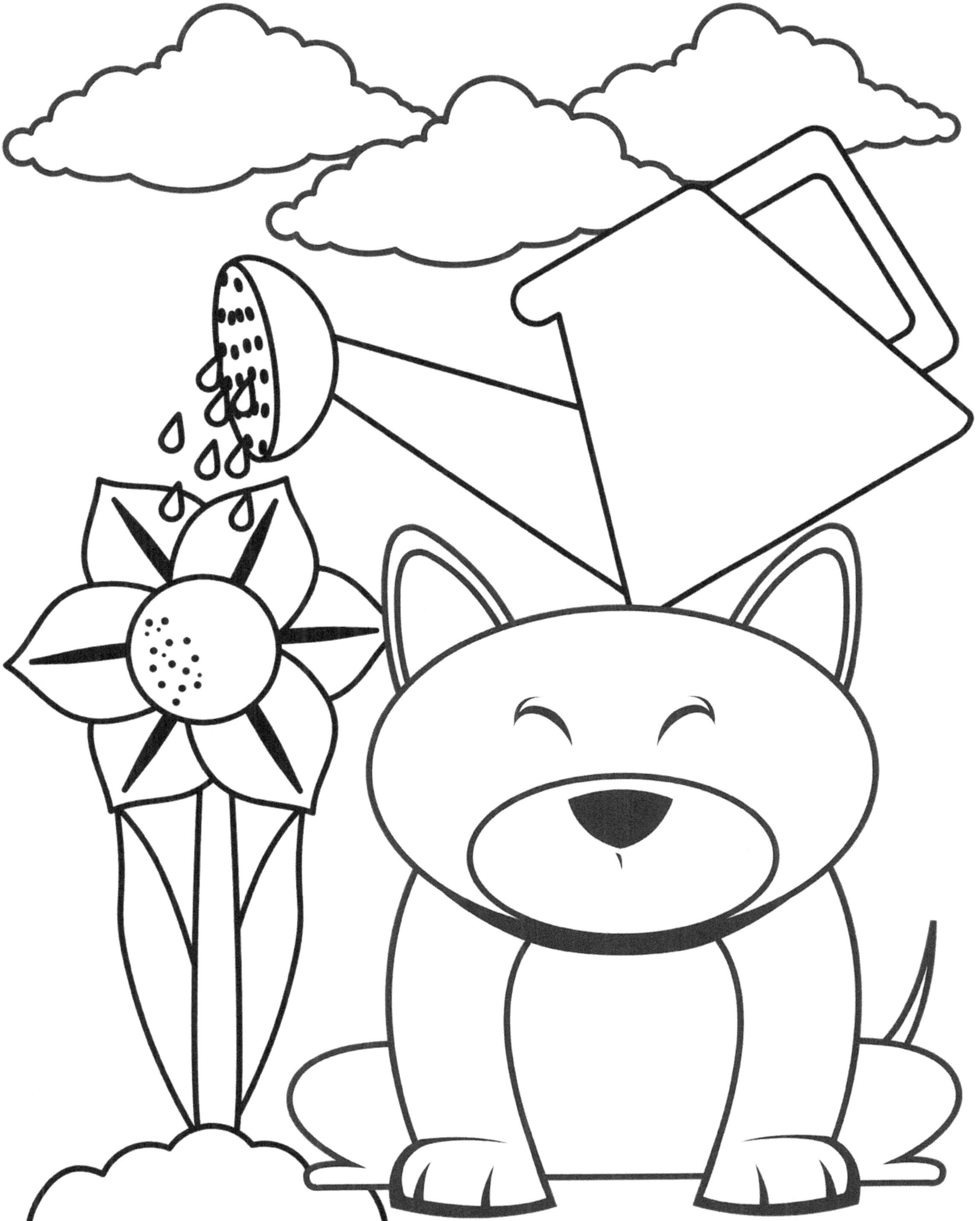

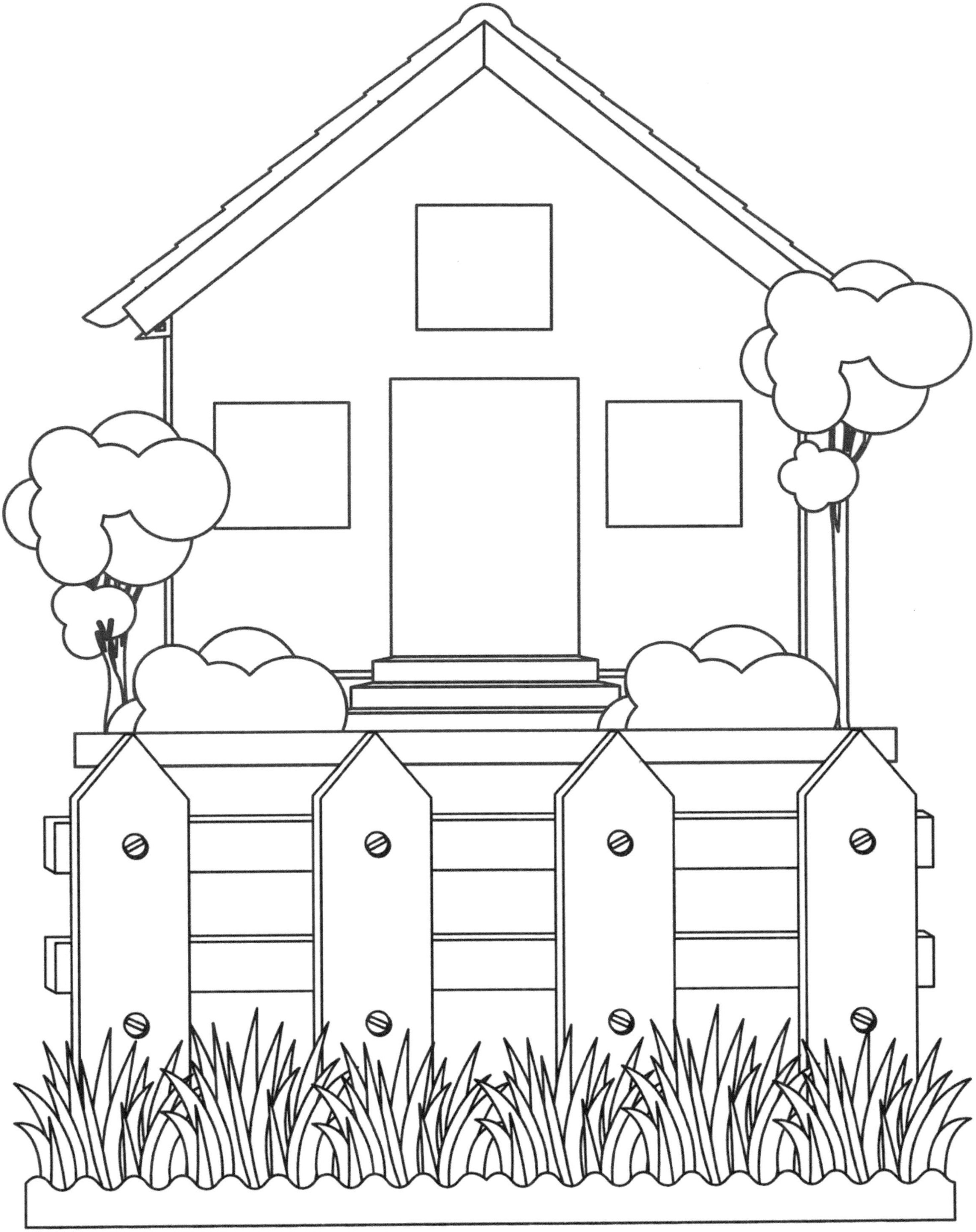

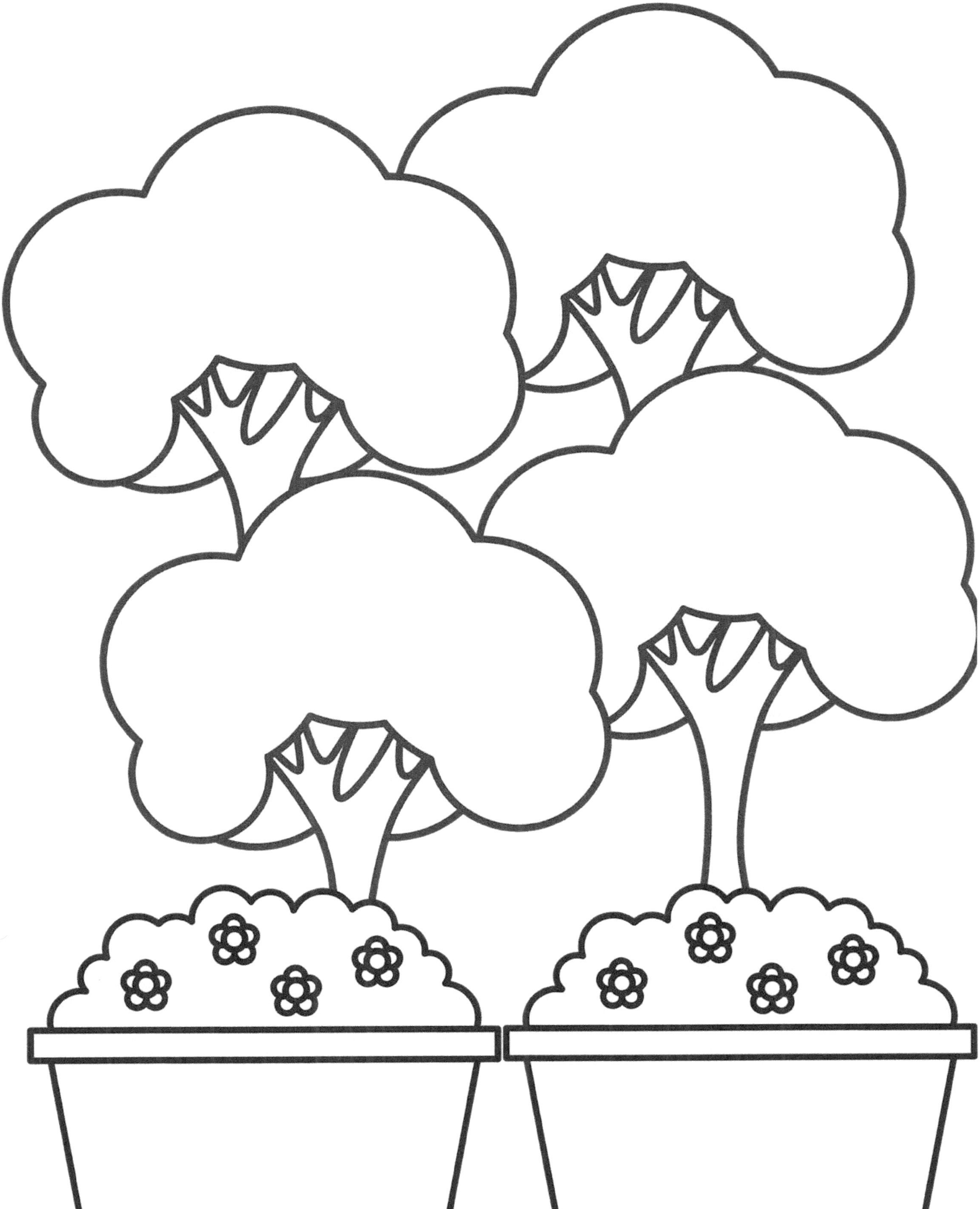

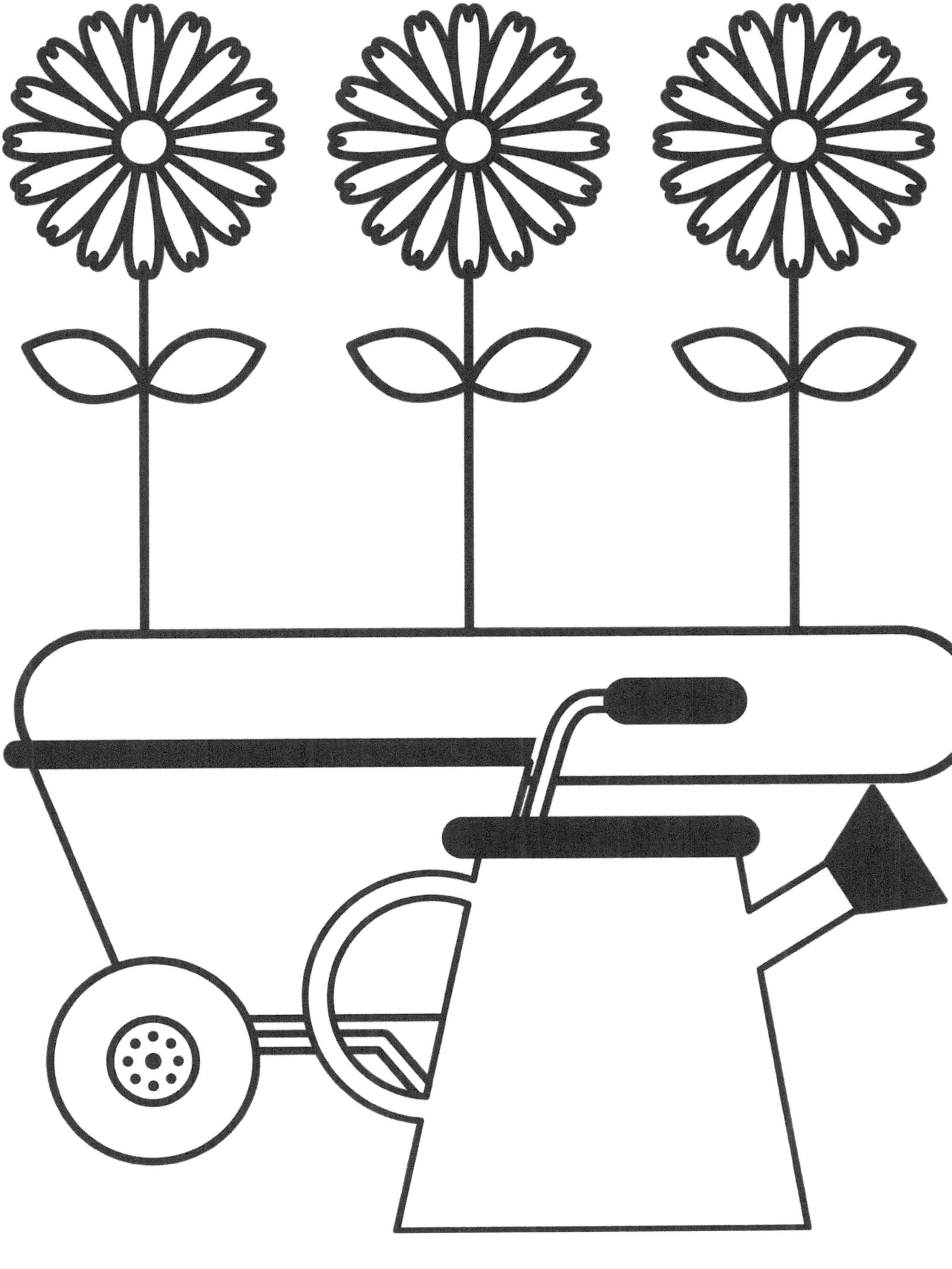

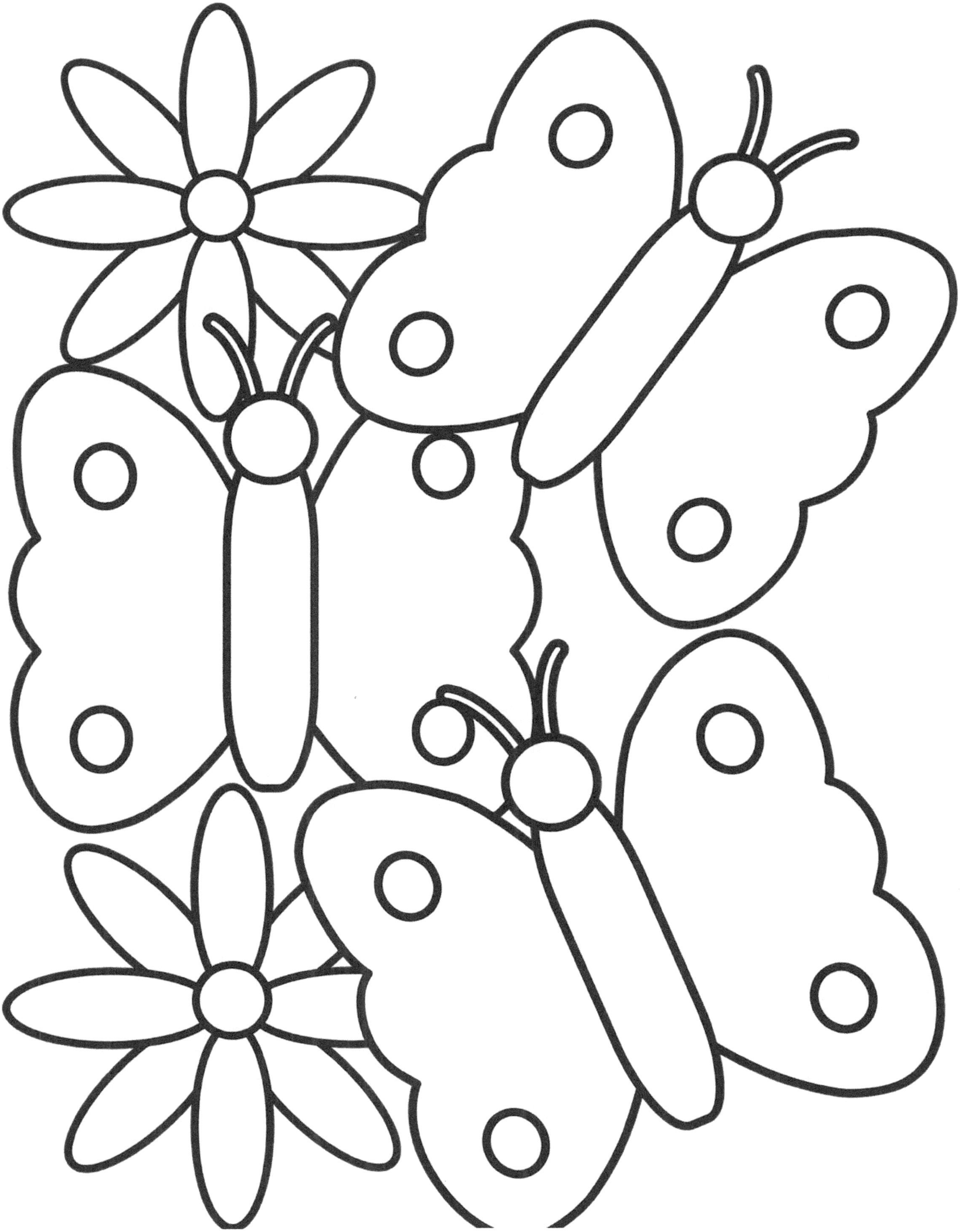

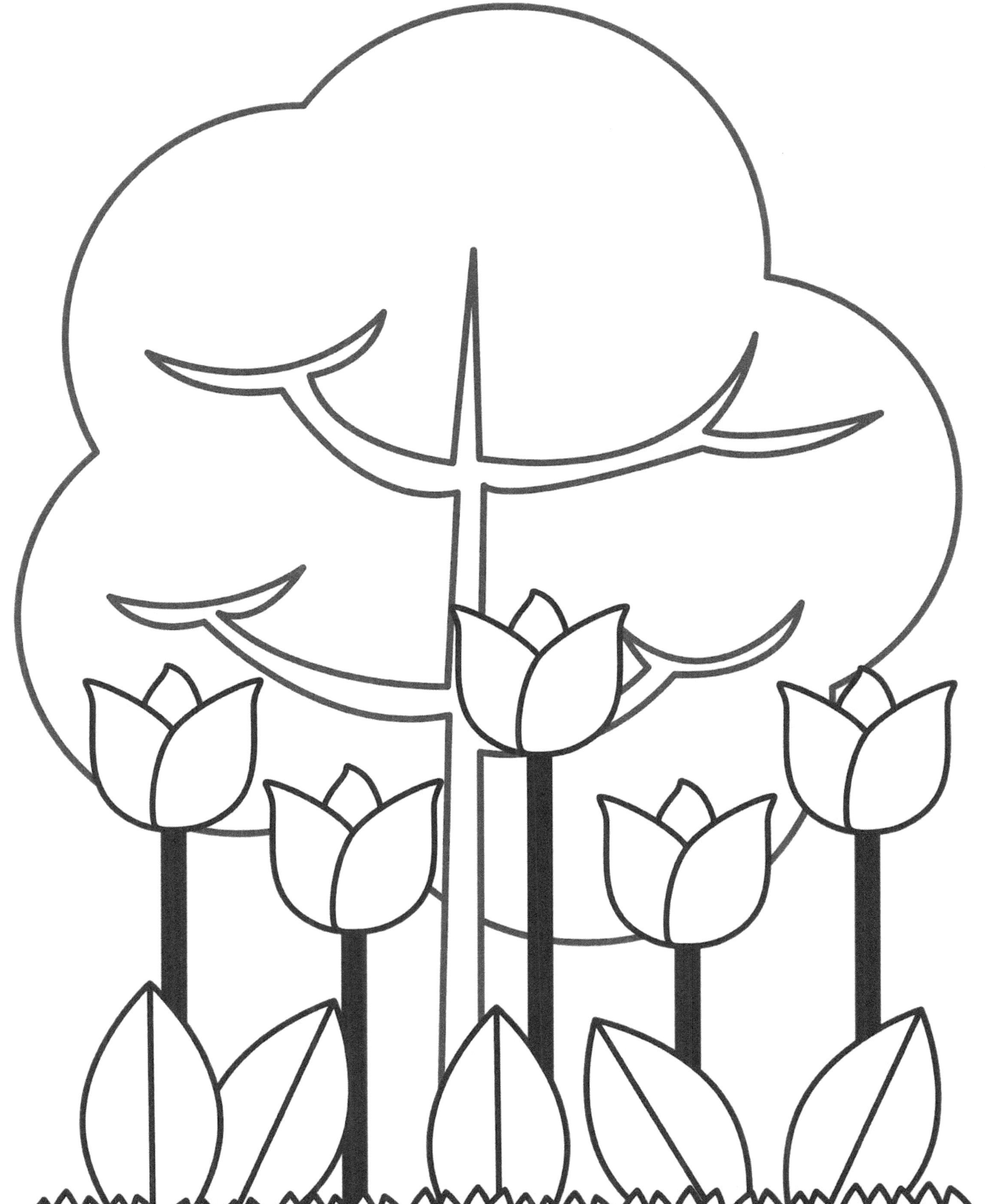

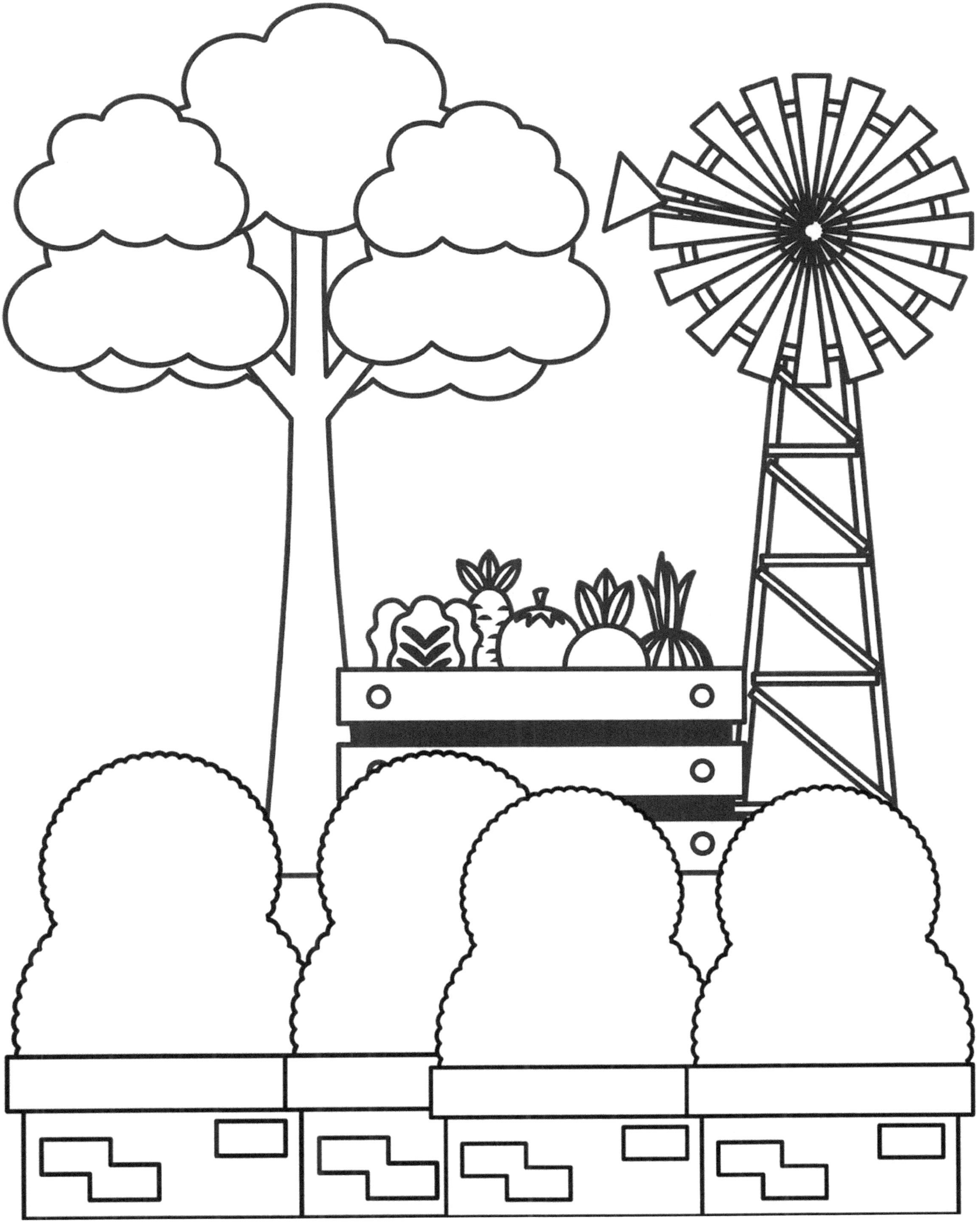

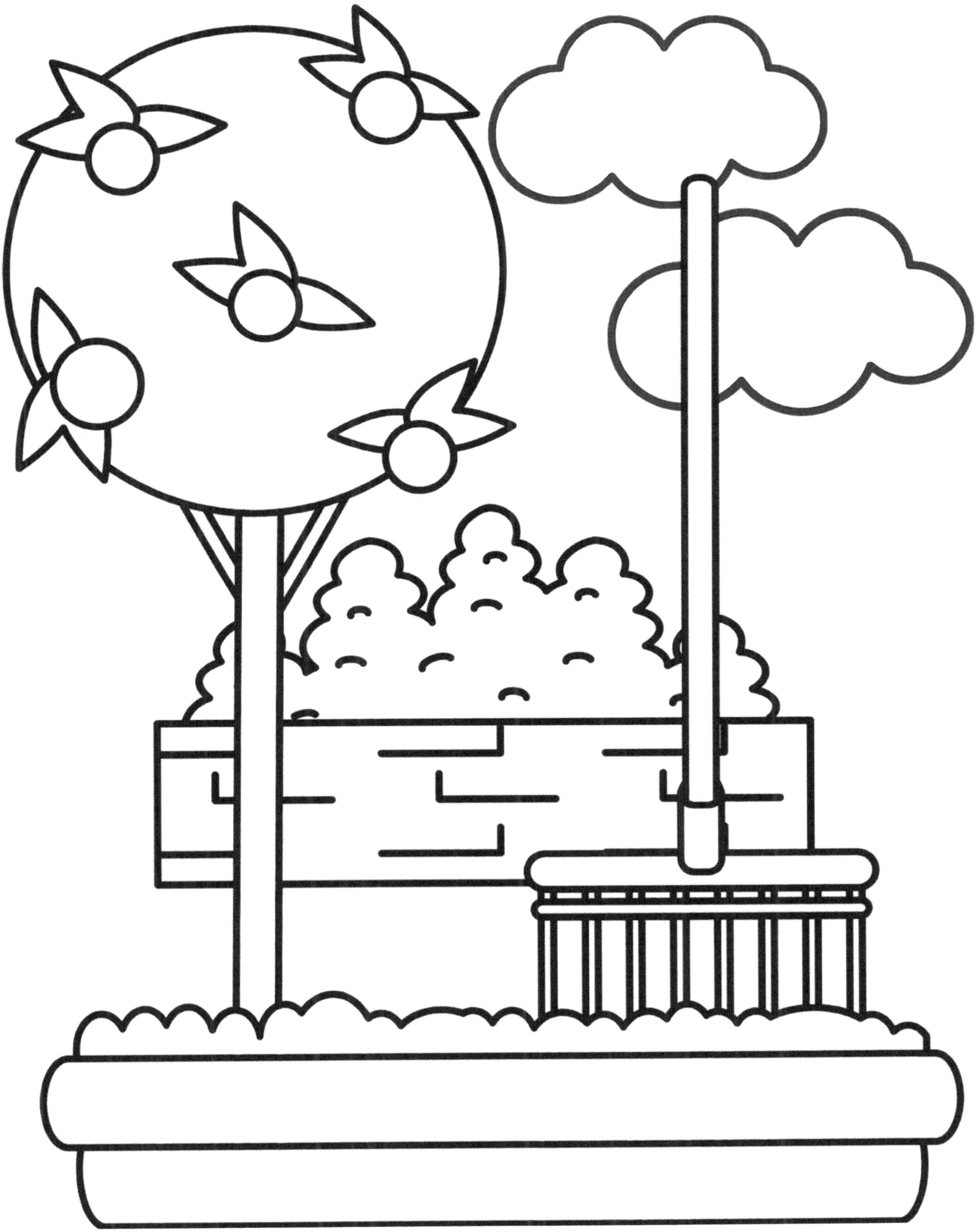

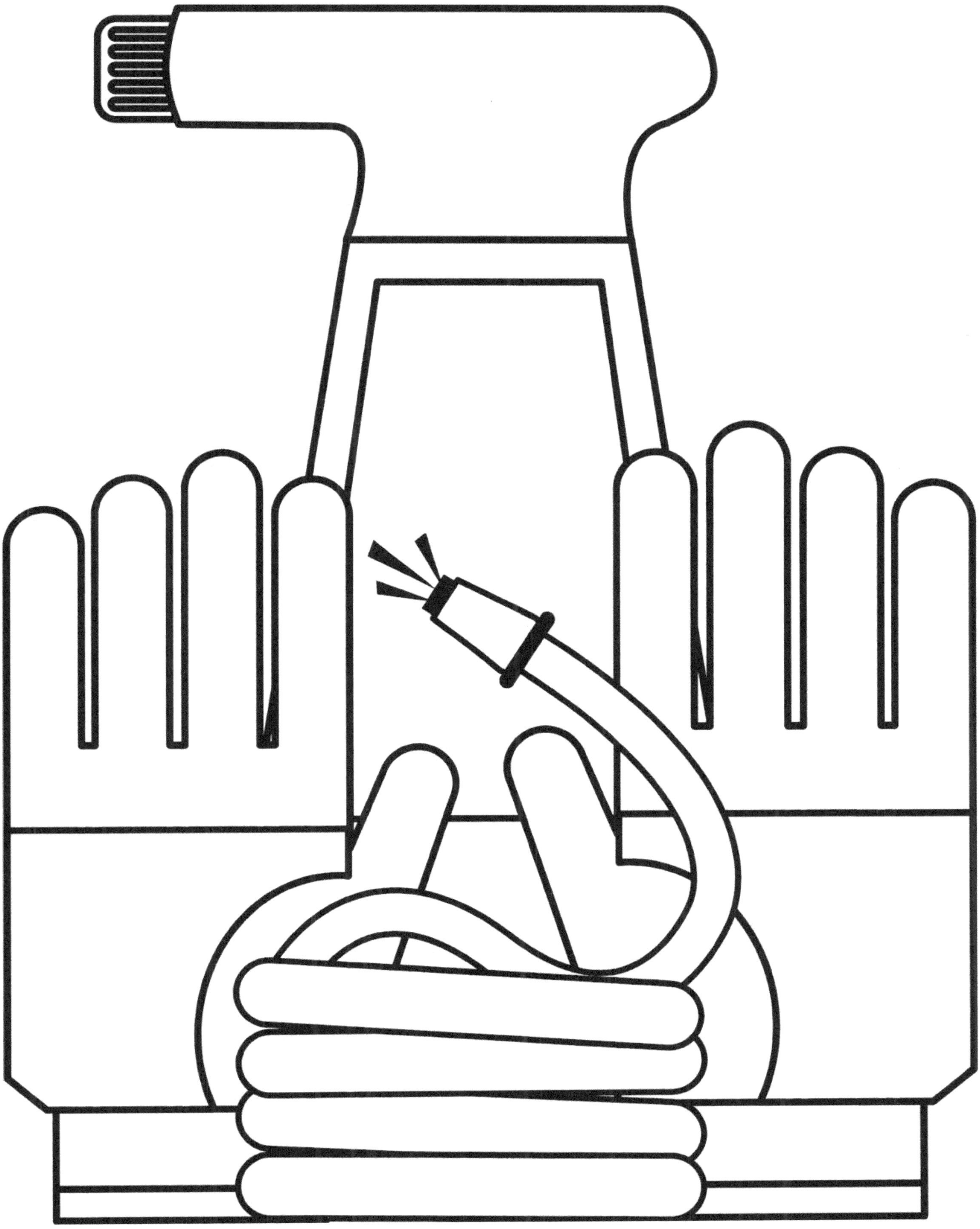

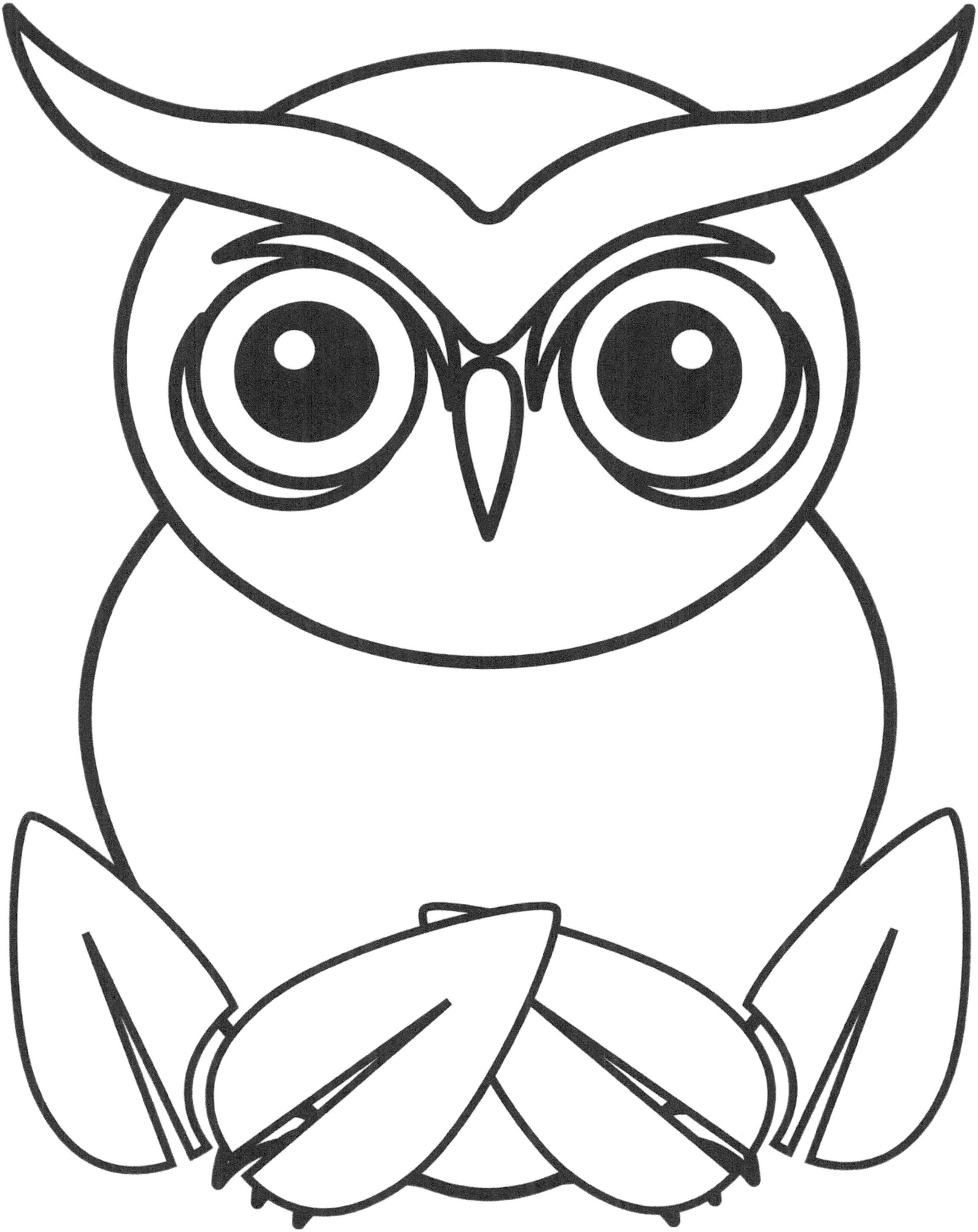

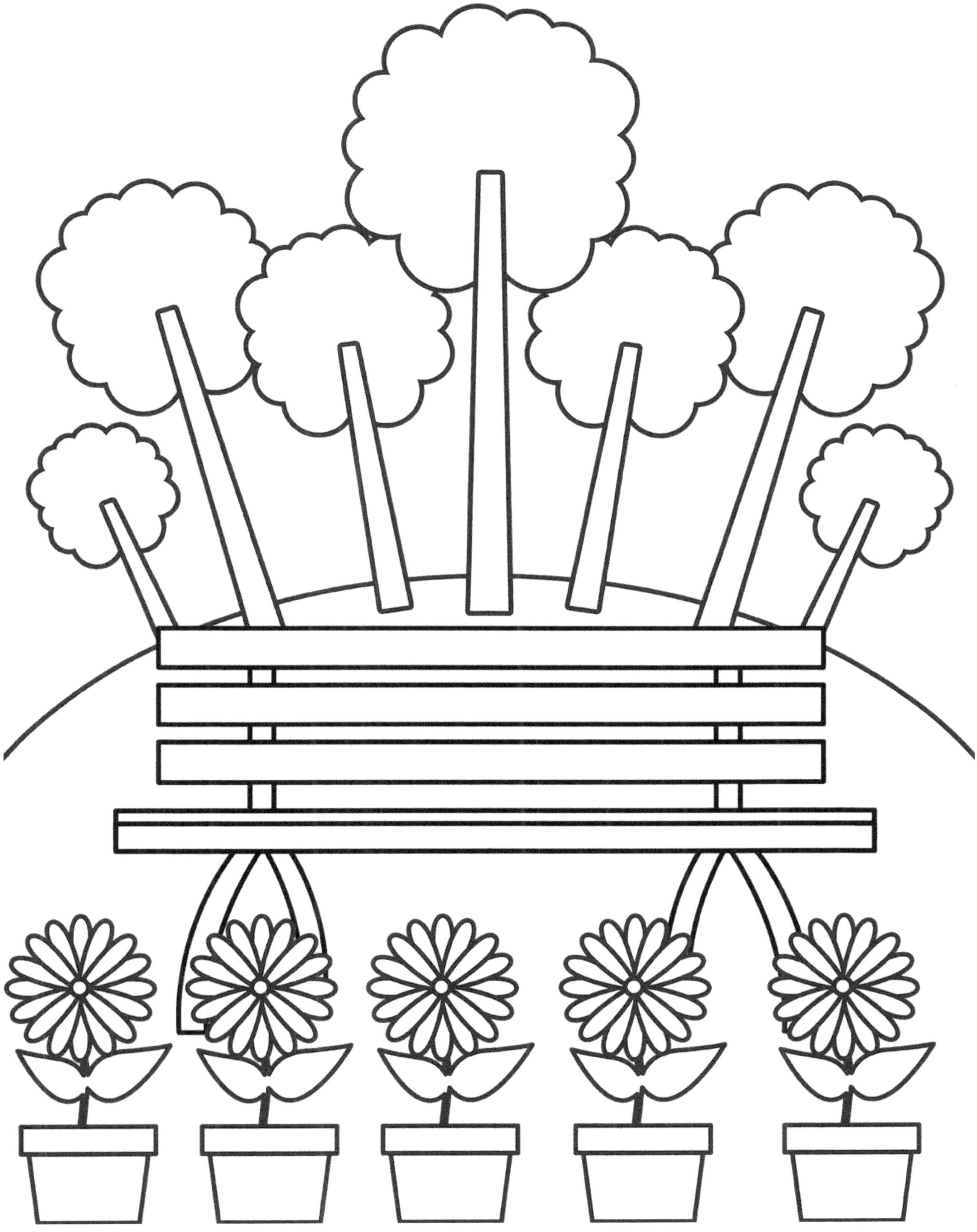

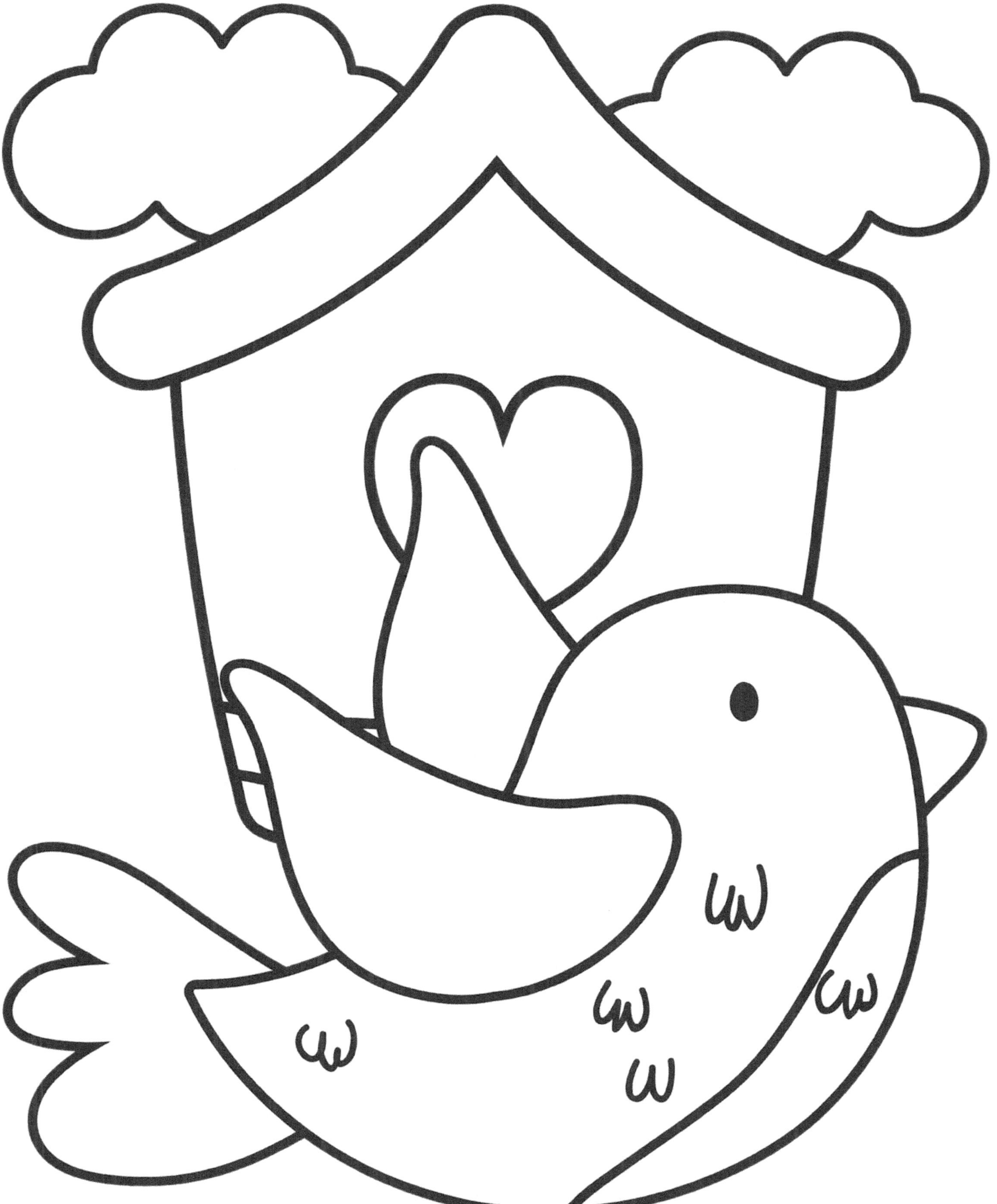

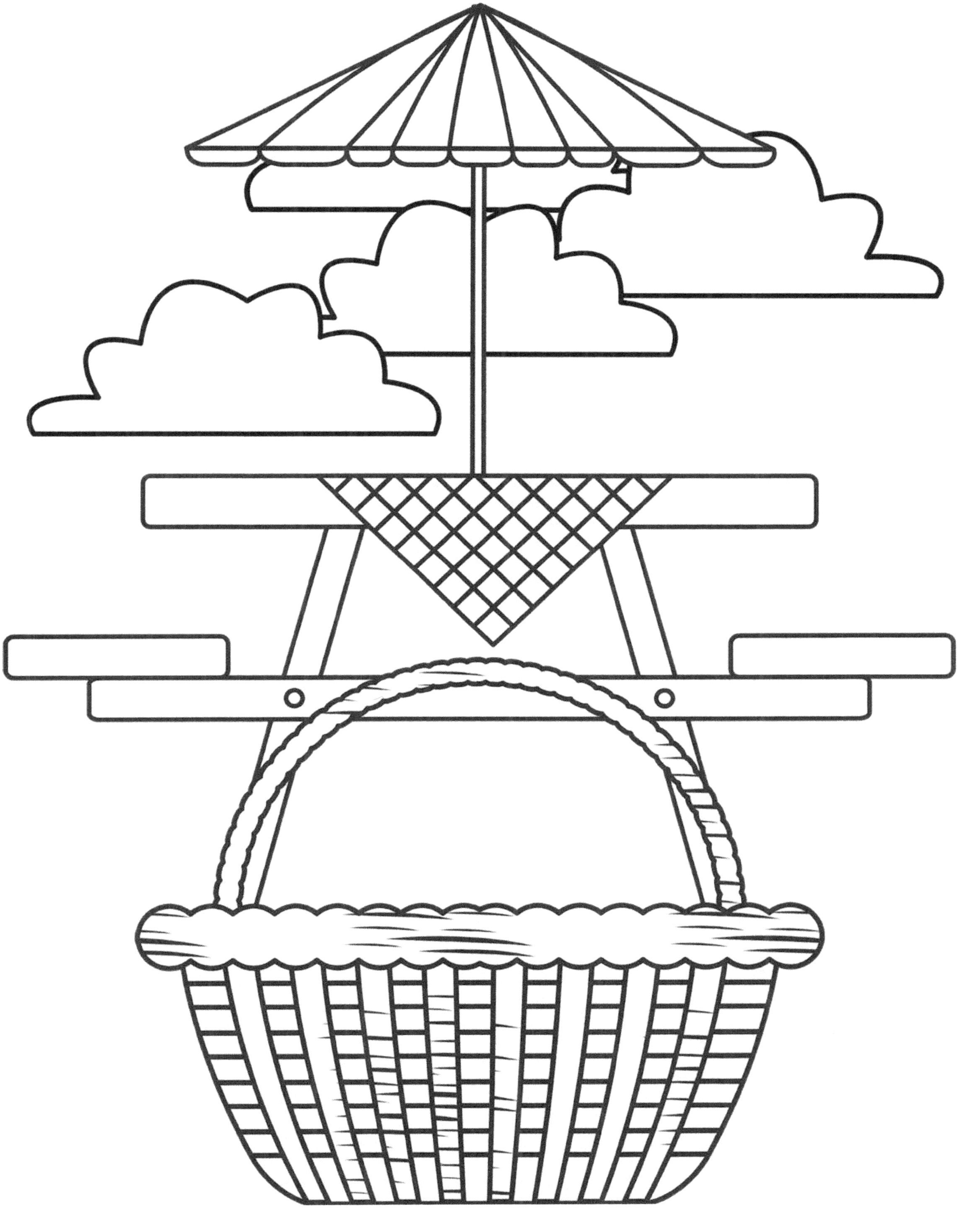

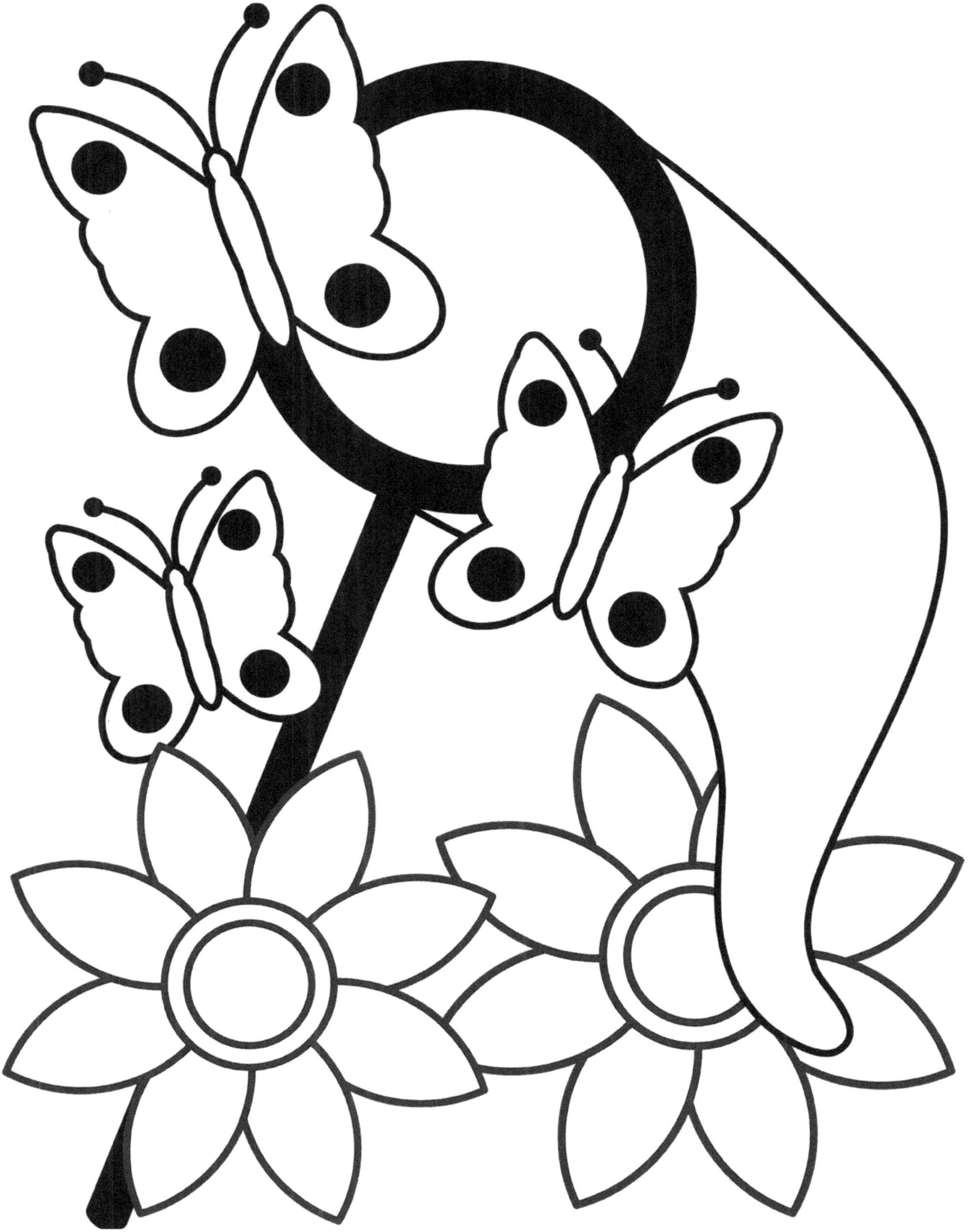

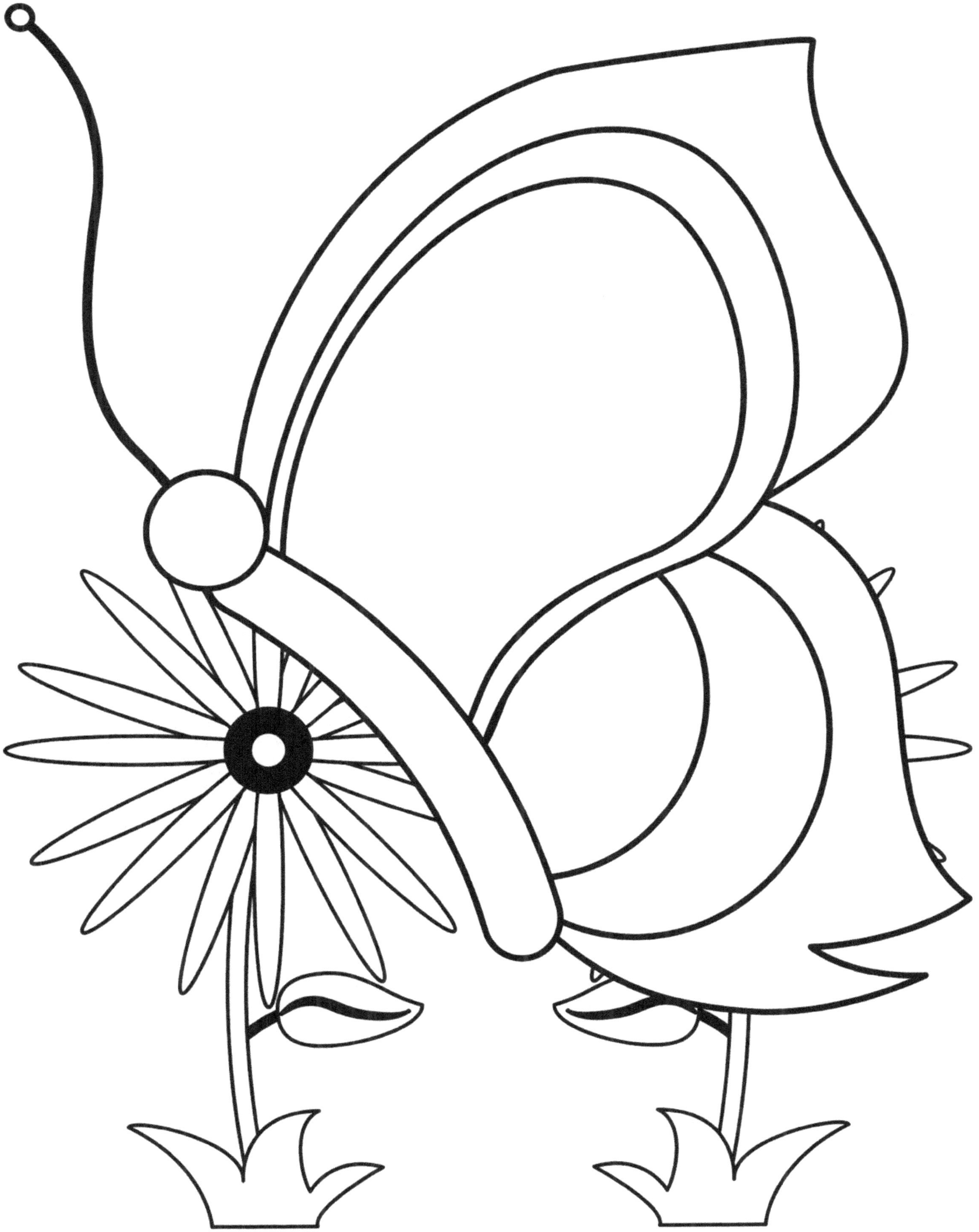

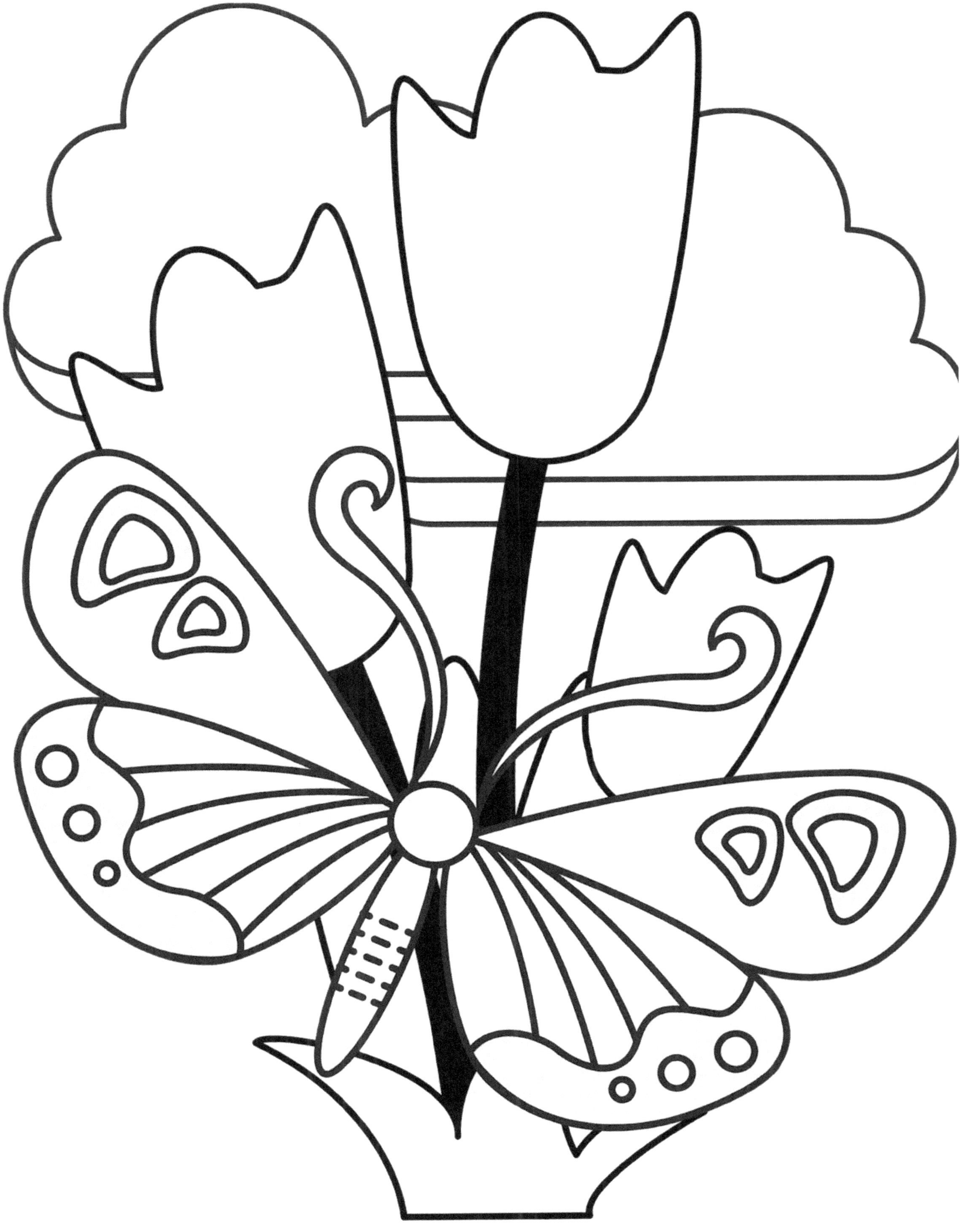

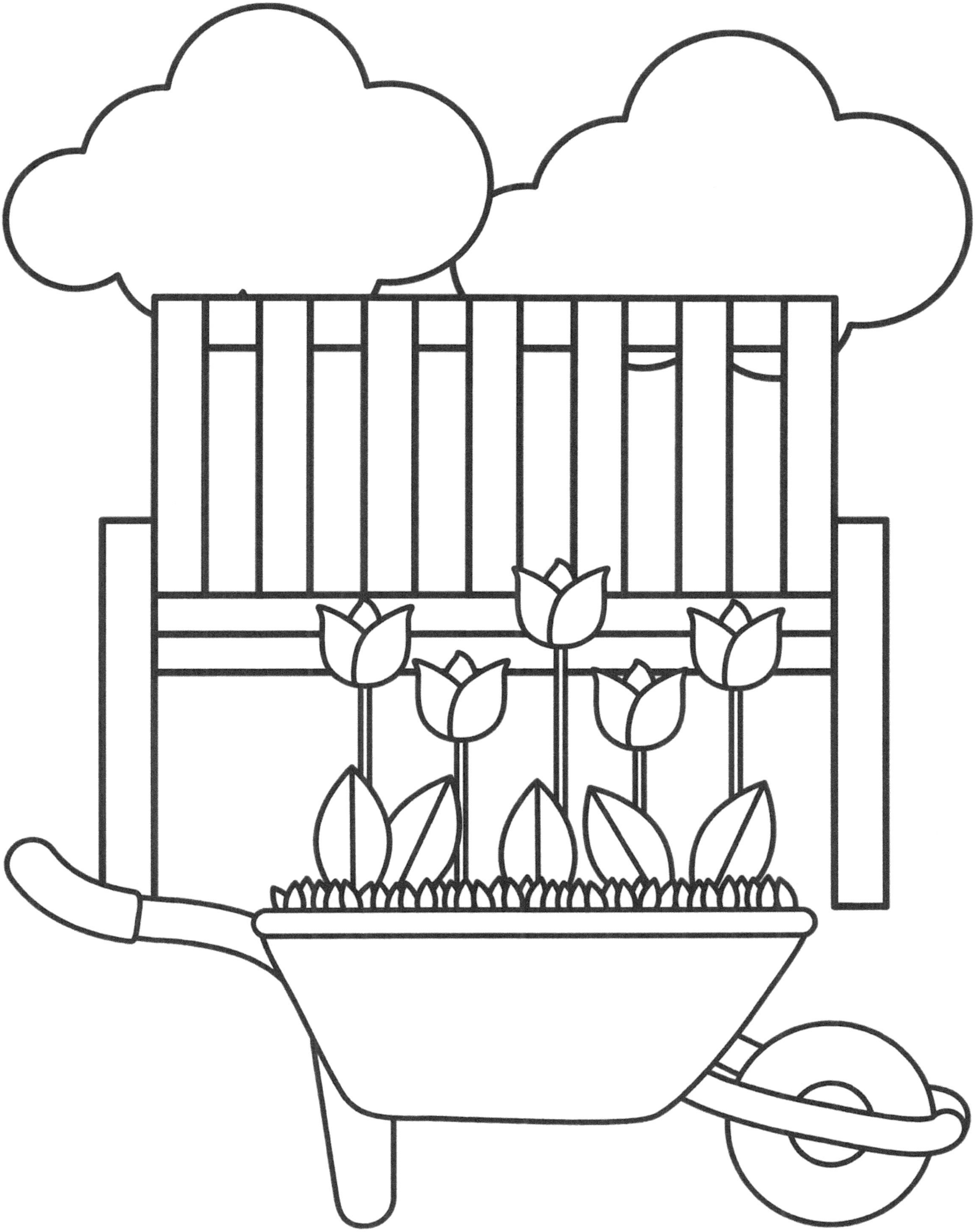

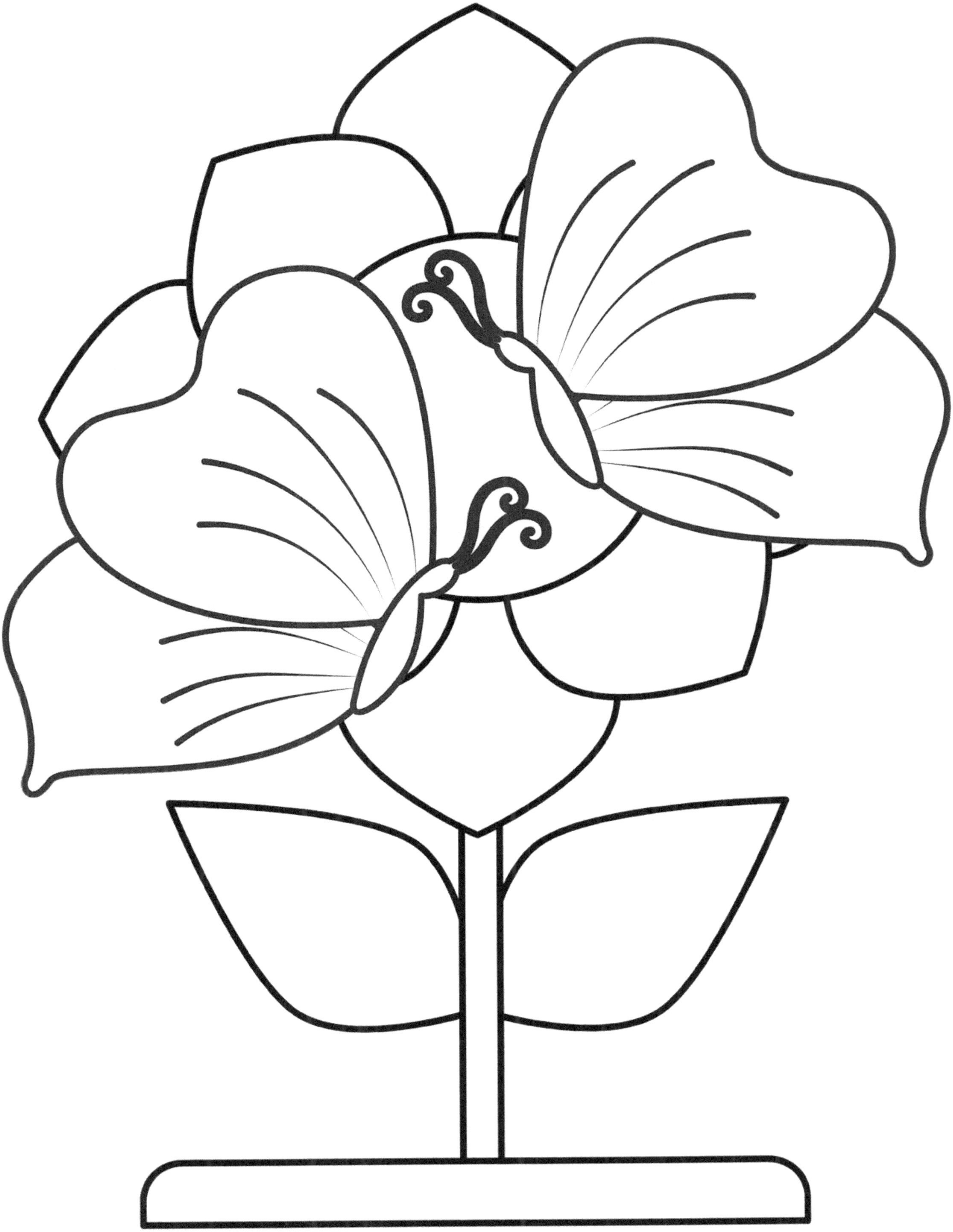

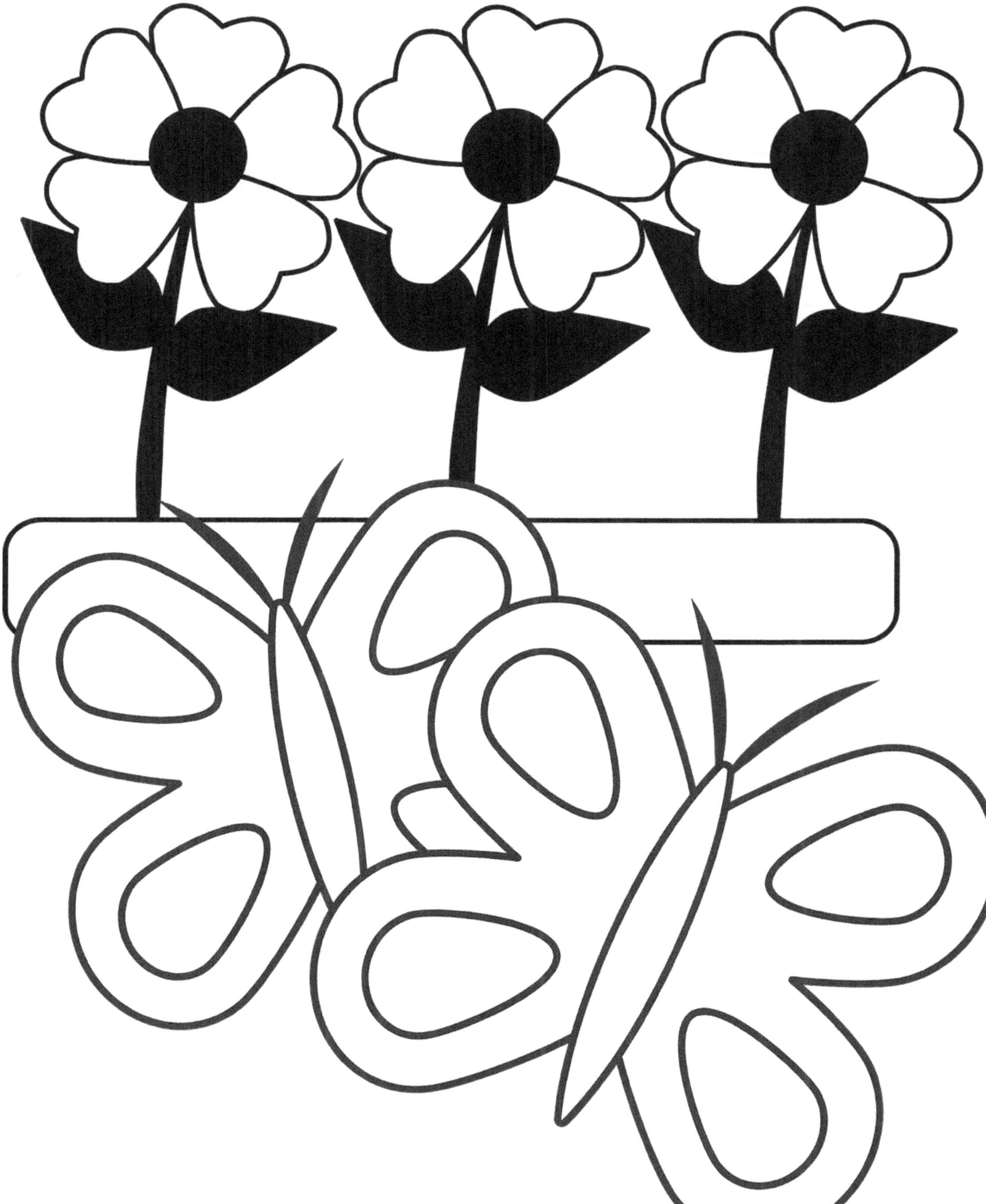

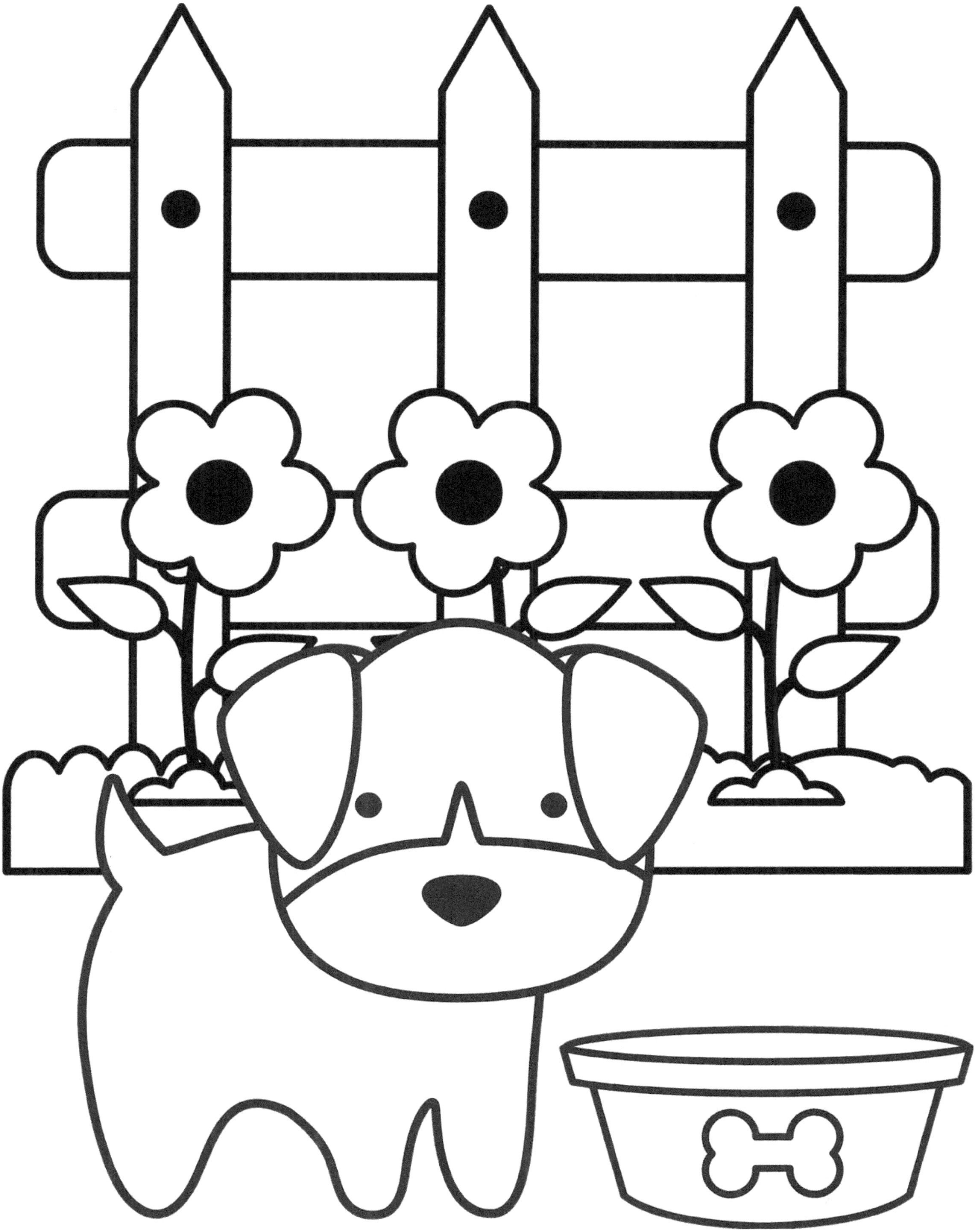

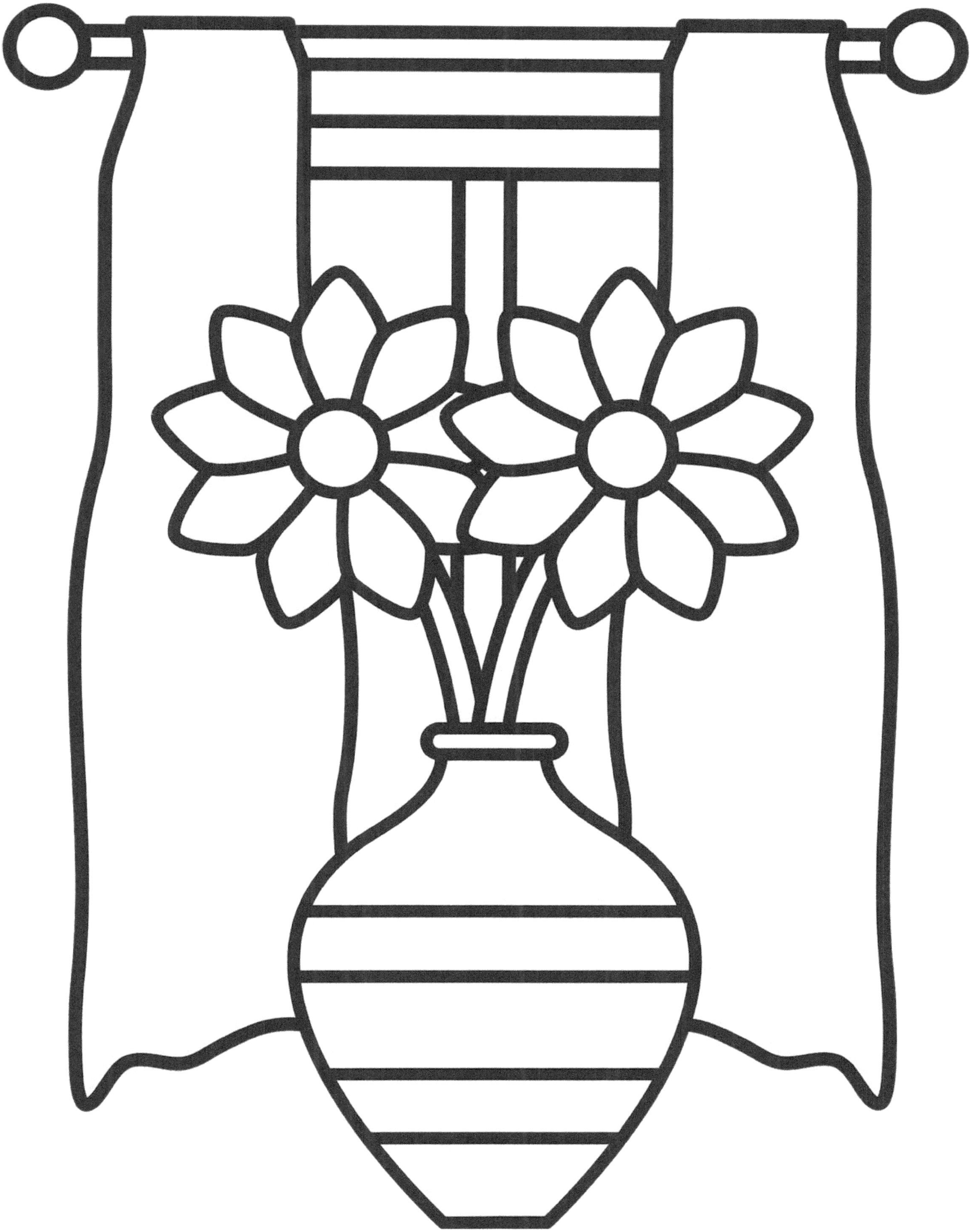

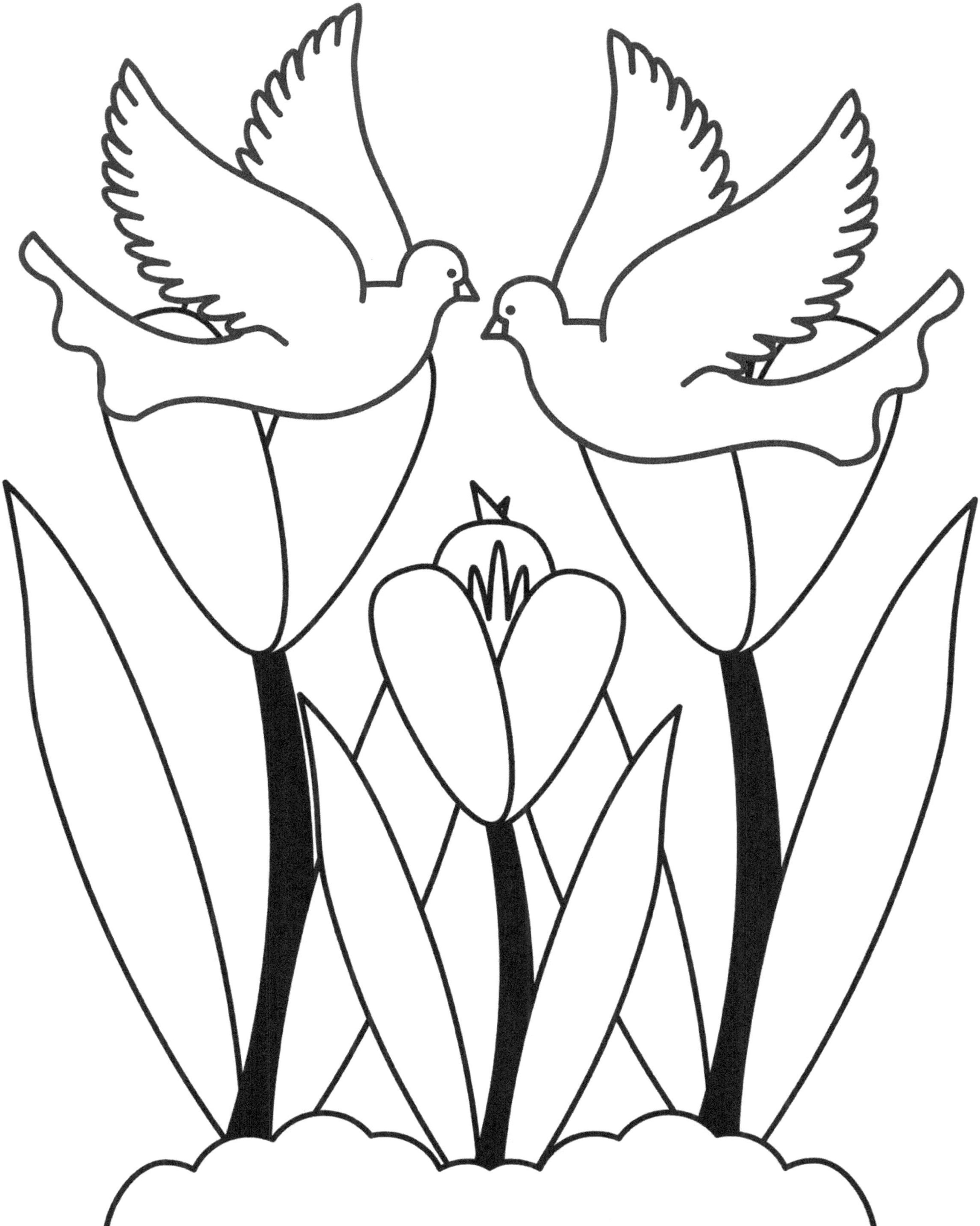

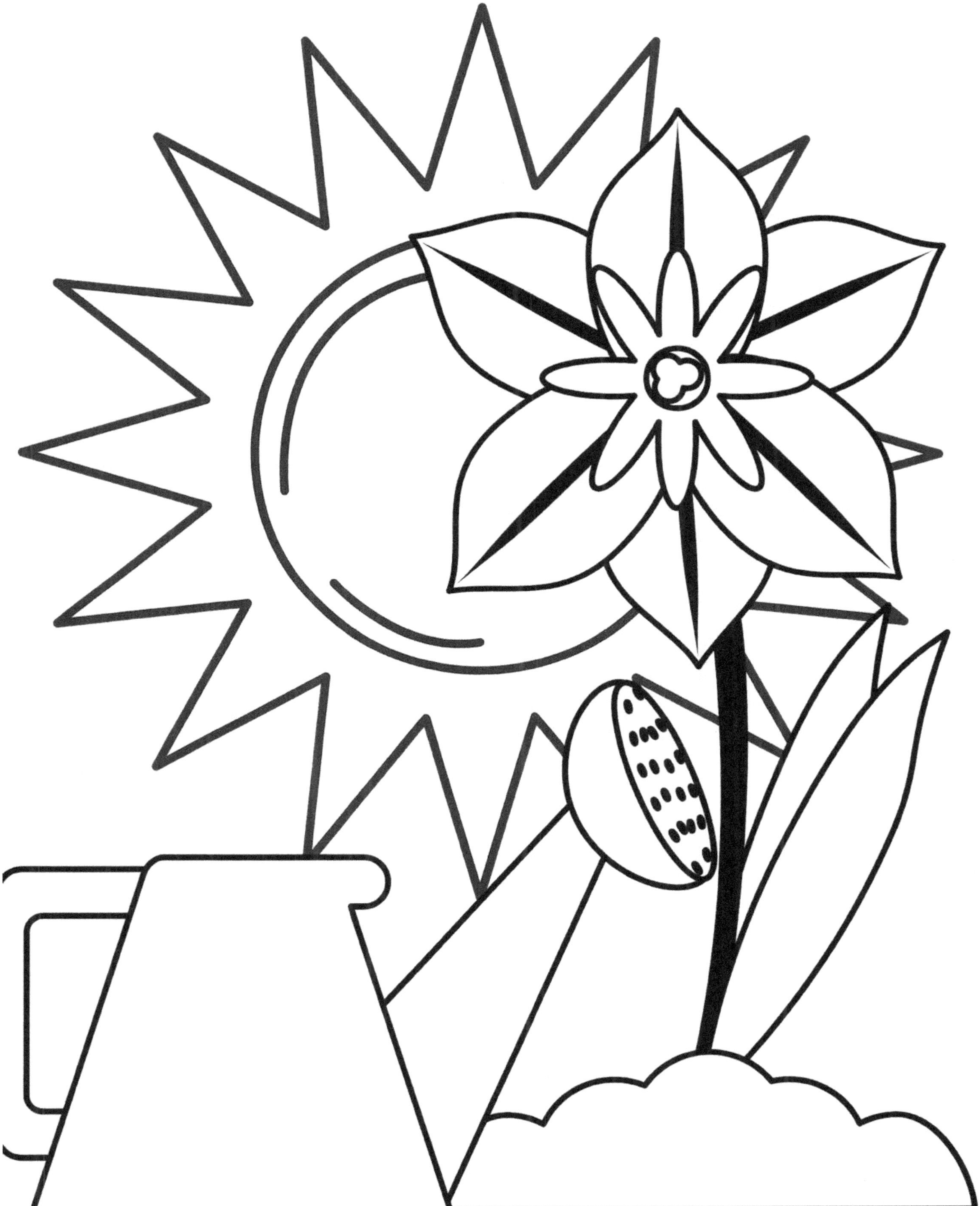

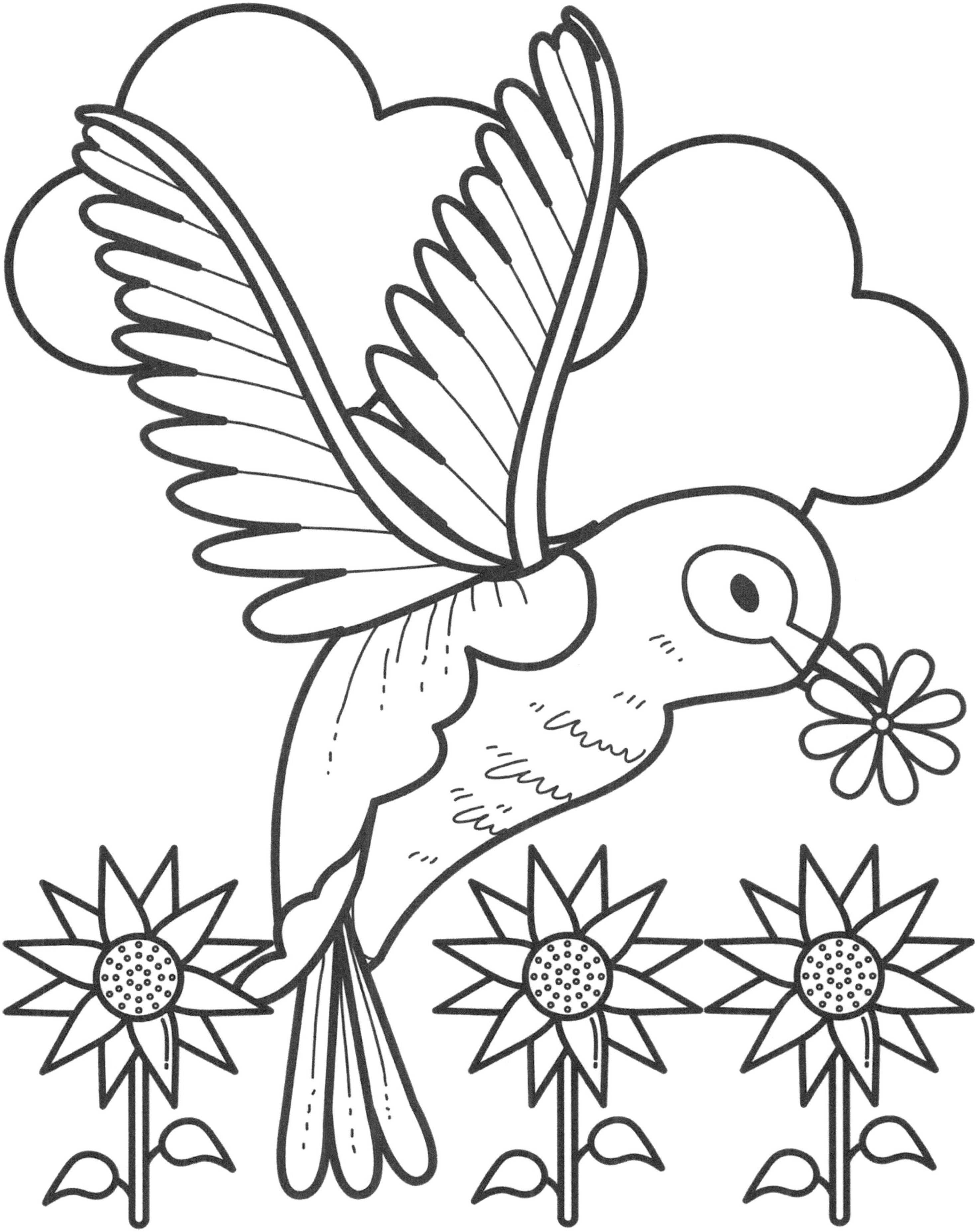

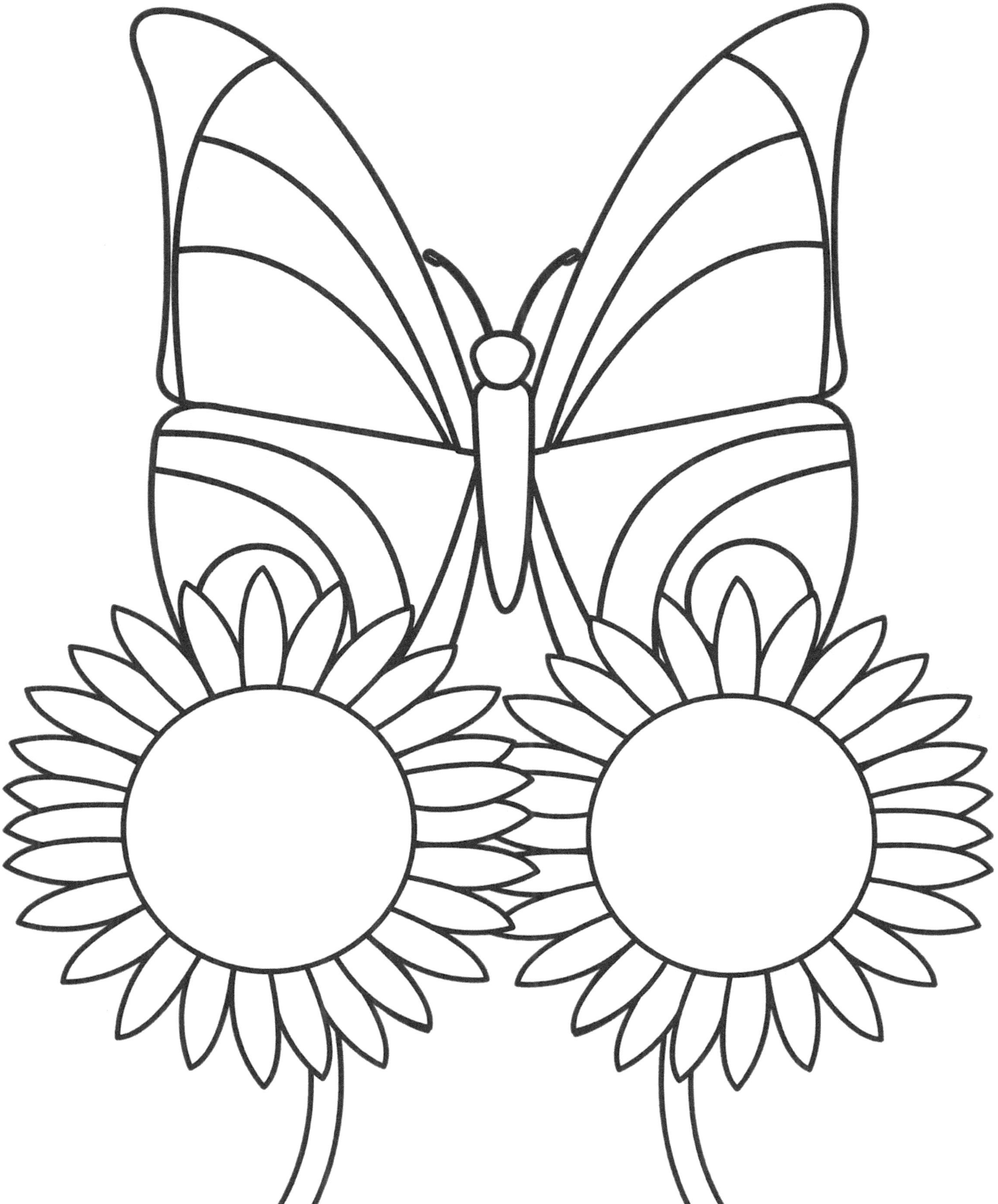

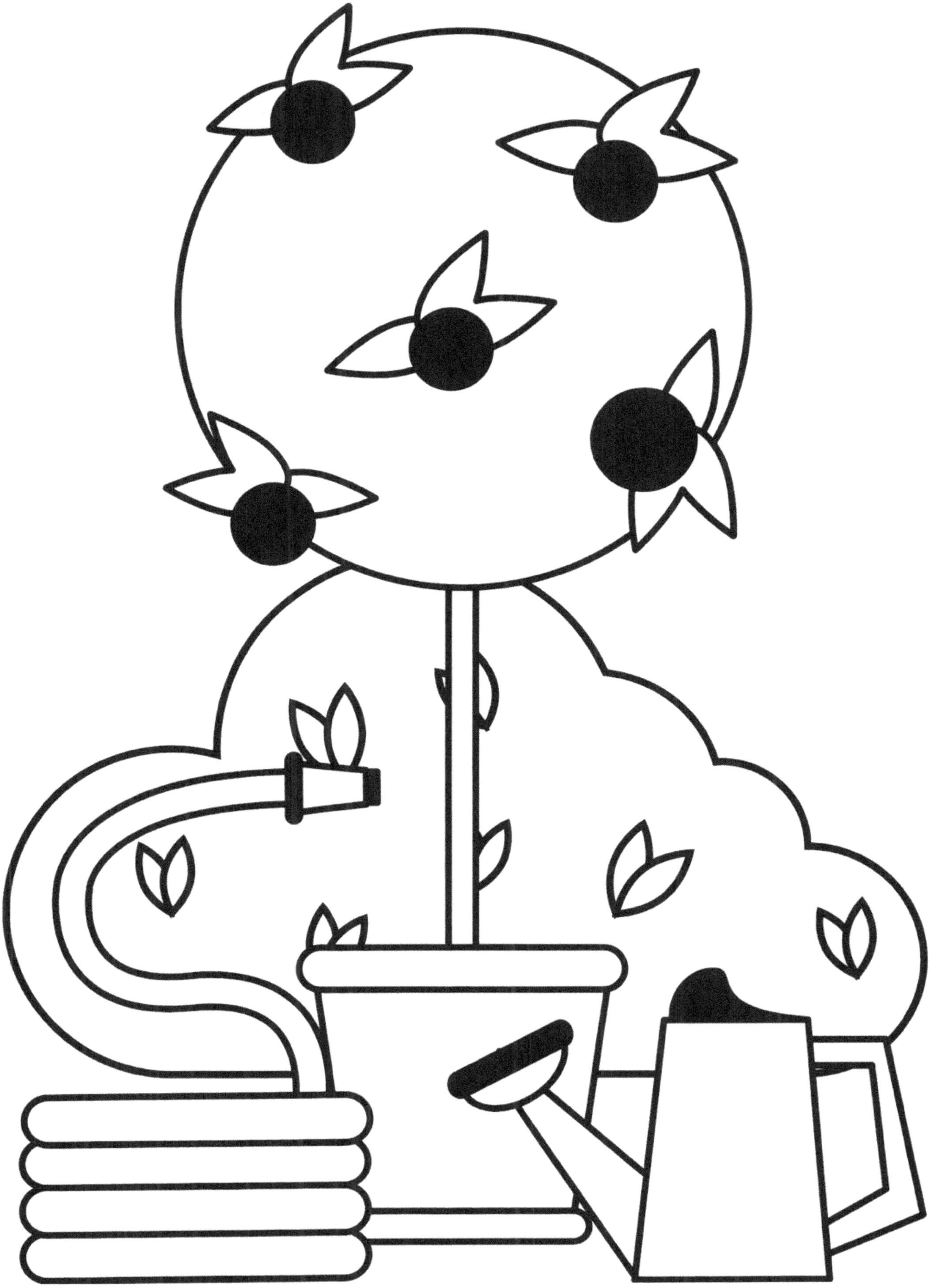

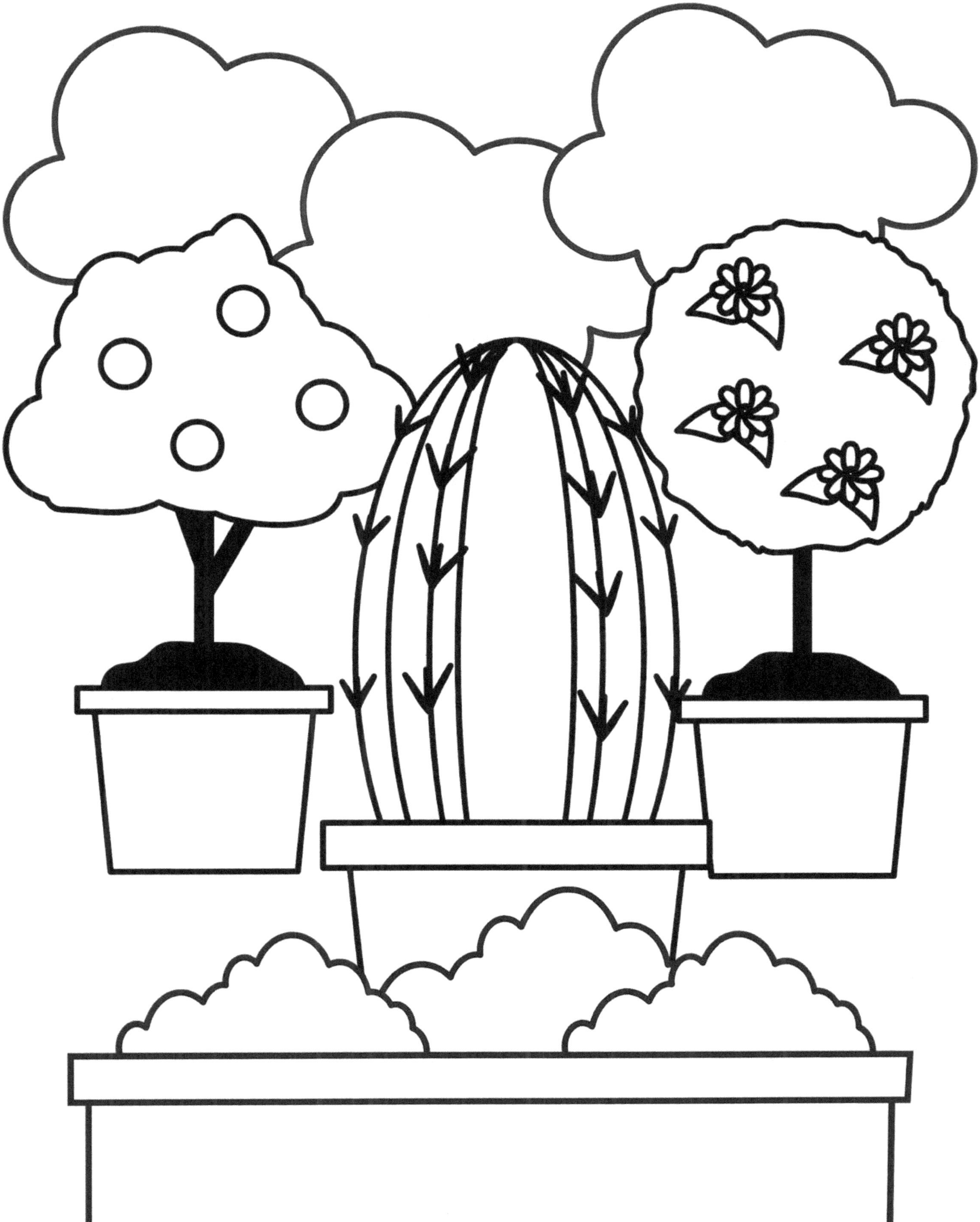

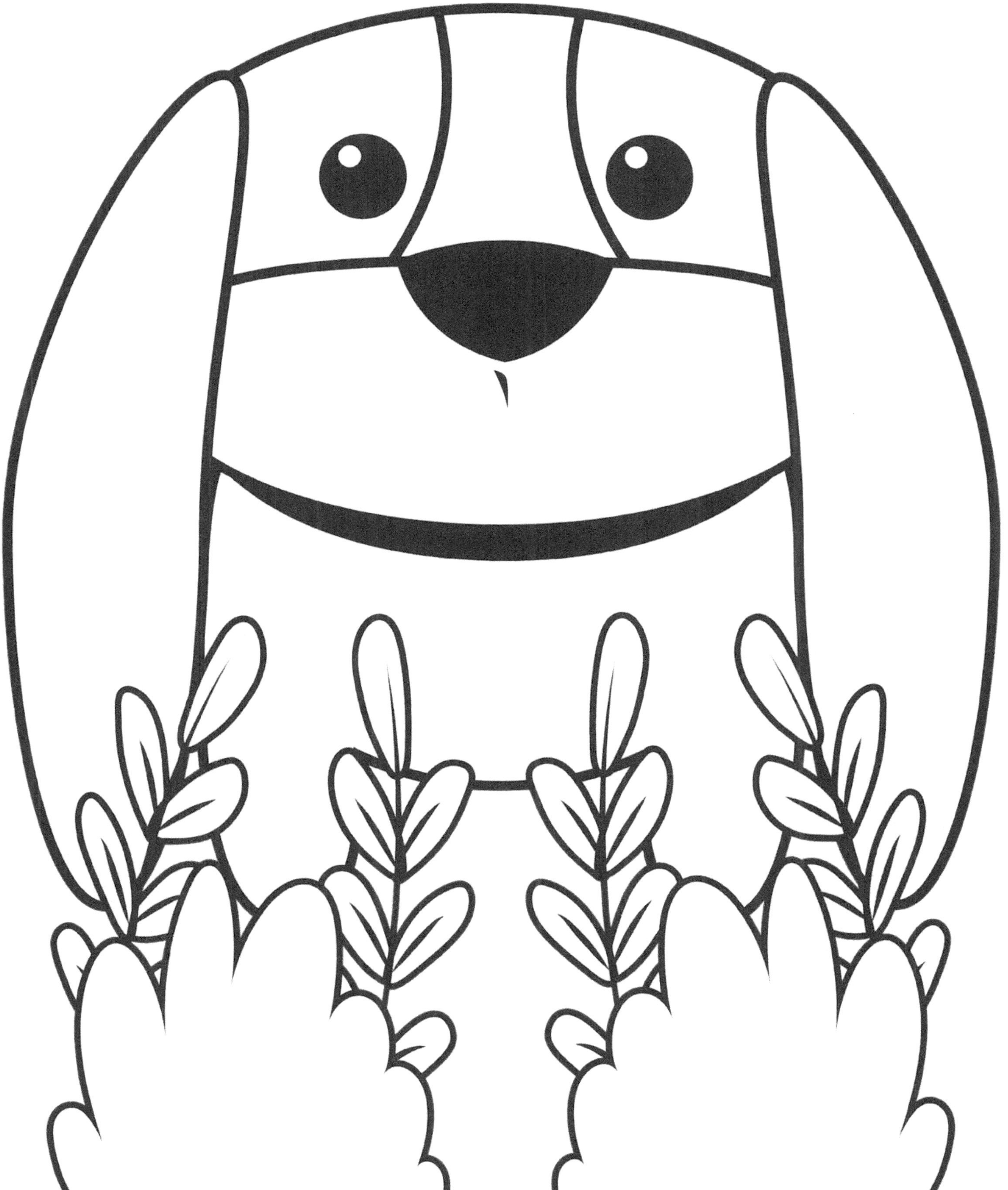

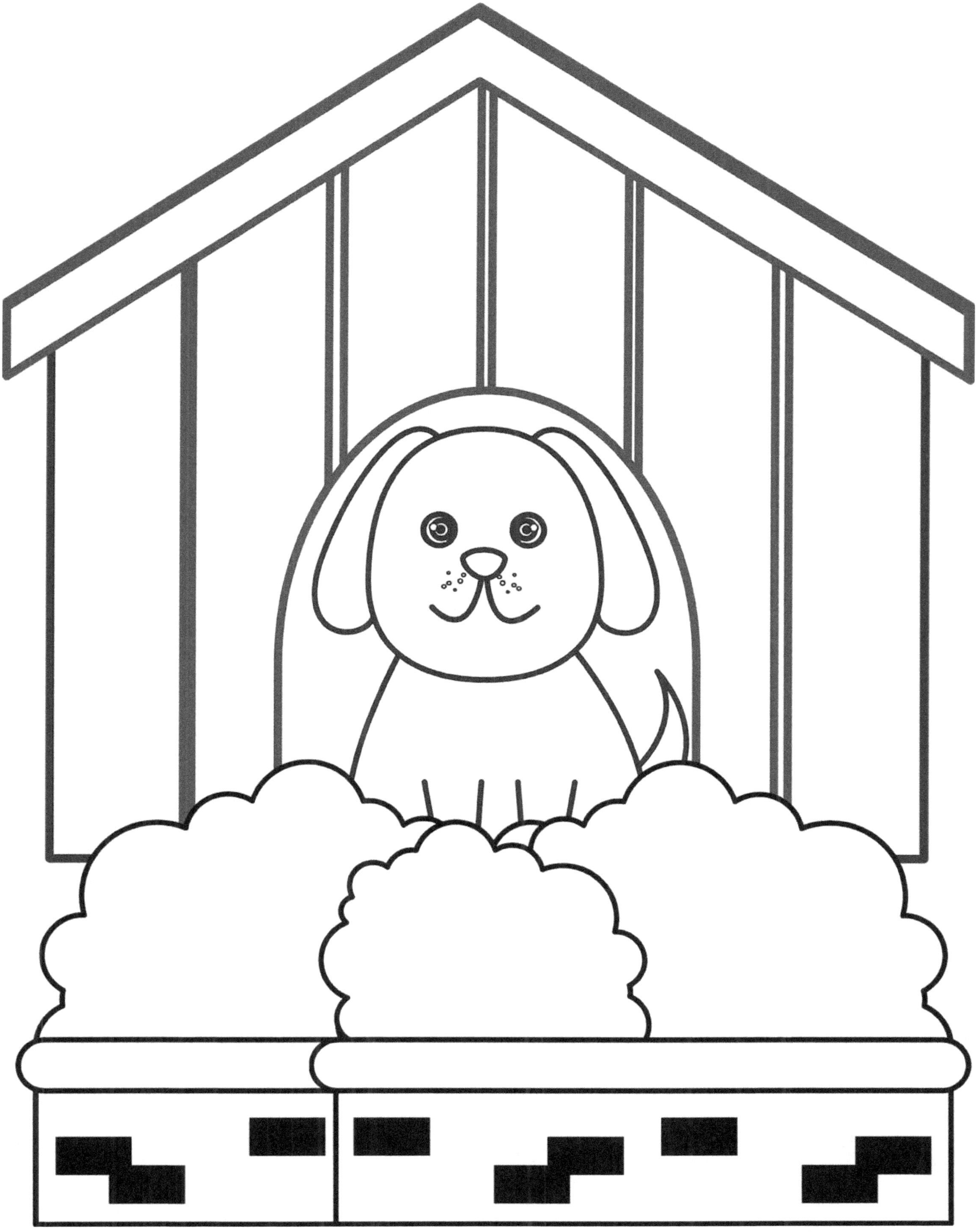

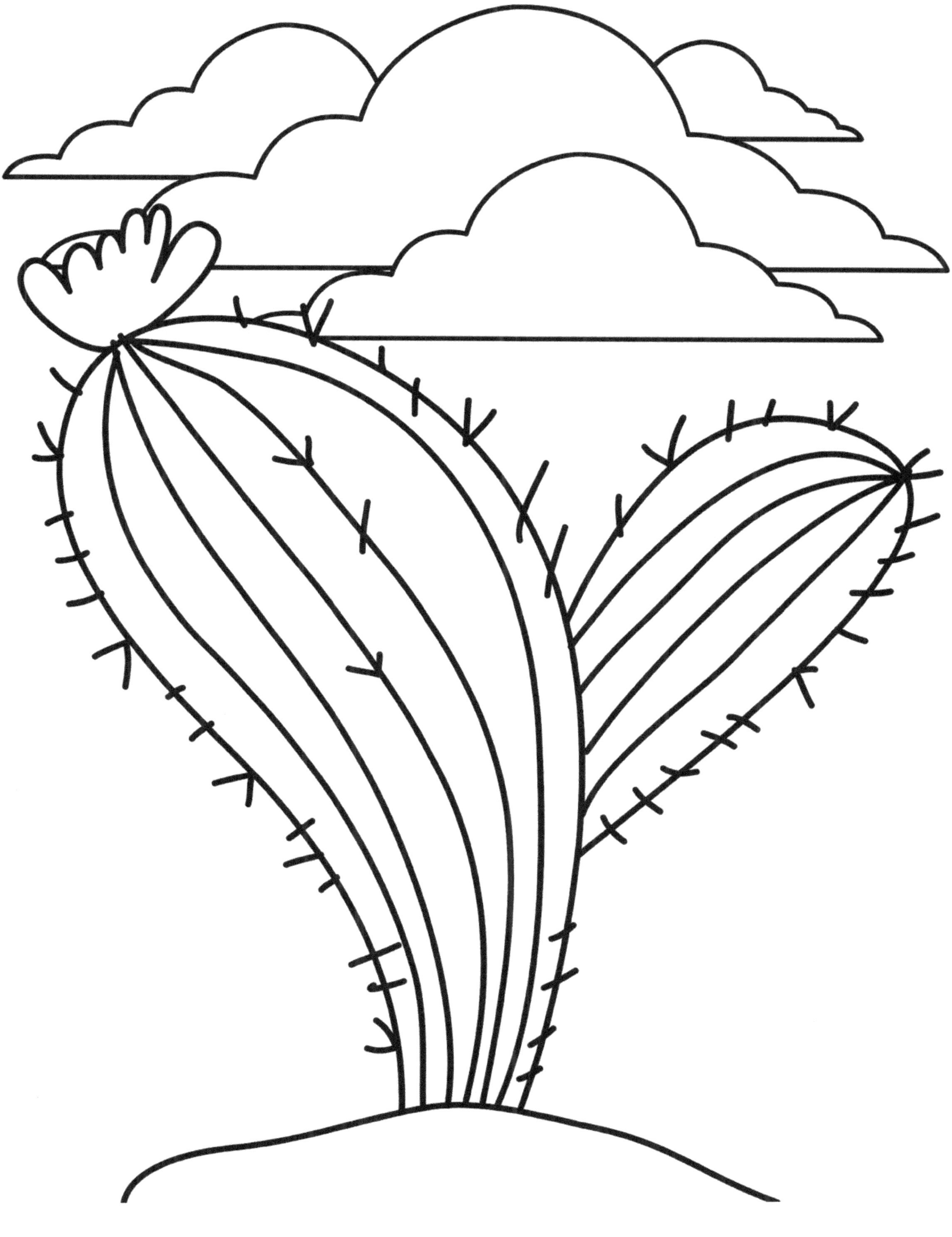

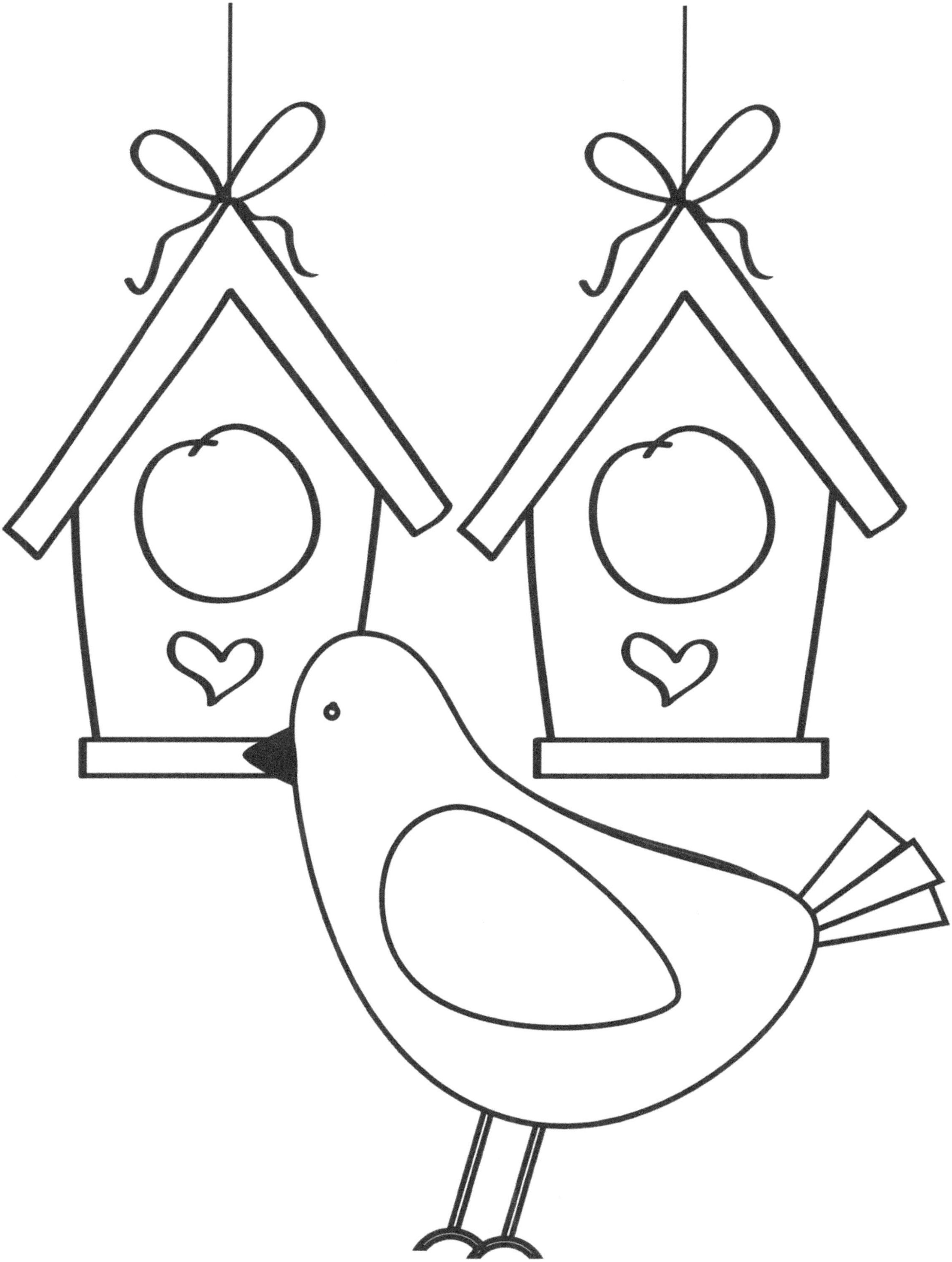

ISBN: 9798585547928

www.ingramcontent.com/pod-product-compliance
Lightning Source LLC
Chambersburg PA
CBHW080614220526
45466CB00010B/3342
9798585547928